Manchester-born David [illegible] ry Bank Mill as a young [illegible] us summer's day out in rural Cheshire. At the time he had no idea that once young children had worked behind those looming walls and it wasn't until thirty years later that he was to return and discover the truth about those children. In 2011 David was employed by Darlow Smithson Productions as a story finder, tasked with researching the archive at Quarry Bank to discover real people and events that the series' writers could adapt to create a drama series.

David's passion was ignited, and since then, with the help of the National Trust team and the many volunteer researchers at the archive, he has become an expert on the history of Quarry Bank Mill and neighbouring Styal village and worked as a consultant on the television series.

David has enjoyed a long and successful career in television drama, as a script writer and producer, working on series such as *Grange Hill*, *Brookside*, *Hollyoaks*, and *Coronation Street*, and is the author of *Access All Areas: Coronation Street*.

Children of

THE MILL

TRUE STORIES FROM QUARRY BANK

David Hanson

headline

First published in 2014 by
HEADLINE PUBLISHING GROUP

First published in paperback in 2015 by
HEADLINE PUBLISHING GROUP

1

Cataloguing in Publication Data is available from the British Library

Paperback ISBN 978 1 4722 2043 1

Typeset in Bembo by Avon DataSet Ltd, Bidford-on-Avon, Warwickshire

Printed and bound in the UK by Clays Ltd, St Ives plc

Plate sections designed by Ben Cracknell Studioes

Archive photographs and paintings courtesy of Quarry Bank Mill © National Trust. Photography from the television series *The Mill* © Ryan McNamara

Headline's policy is to use papers that are natural, renewable and recyclable products and made from wood grown in well-managed forests and other controlled sources. The logging and manufacturing processes are expected to conform to the environmental regulations of the country of origin.

HEADLINE PUBLISHING GROUP
An Hachette UK Company
Carmelite House
50 Victoria Embankment
London EC4Y 0DZ

www.headline.co.uk
www.hachette.co.uk

dsp
an endemol company

This book accompanies the television series *The Mill* created by Darlow Smithson Productions Ltd and filmed at Quarry Bank Mill in Cheshire.

Contents

Introduction

Fragments of memory . . . a hot summer day, a lazy, aimless stroll along a meandering river bank, the air thick with the droning of bees. A hiatus in my life, university drop-out, nothing better to do . . . Young lads of eleven or twelve gripping a fraying, many-knotted rope and launching themselves off a high grassy bank above a turgid, oily river – seeming to hang in space in clouds of lazy insects and dust before plunging gleefully into the water. A sticky walk along a dusty path with the sweetest of summer breezes stirring the leaves over my head, and then the sound of roaring water, around the next bend. An idyll in rural Cheshire, a day that could have happened in any of the last hundred years, apart from the modern camera slung around my neck. Then, as I reached the source of the water's disturbance, a curving weir, I remember looking up and being startled by the sight of a huge building, high and long, looming through a screen of the tallest oaks and beeches, its thousands of tiny windows blinking in the glare. An enormous mill, sitting incongruously in deepest woodland, a relic of the past. I was intrigued, but the day was too glorious to waste exploring what was bound to be a stiflingly hot and oppressive old building. So I passed on by.

What I didn't know was that behind those forbidding walls, long ago, children the age of those carefree boys and even younger worked their lives out in relentless, grinding labour. It wasn't until thirty years later that I began to learn the truth of Quarry Bank Mill.

On another hot summer's day, in August 2012, I was facing those towering mill walls again, only this time it was my job to go in and explore. It was an unusual job for me. I was used to working in television, as both producer and scriptwriter, but this new task was different, taking me deep into the lives of real people and into the genesis of a television series.

I'd been approached by Emily Dalton of Darlow Smithson Productions, which was in the early stages of seeking a commission from Channel 4 to dramatise the story of Quarry Bank Mill in the nineteenth century. Channel 4 was interested, but there was one vital question: were there sufficient stories of the kind to engage a modern audience? The mill certainly had a long, rich history, and is now a renowned living museum, but could enough engrossing material be excavated from the mill's archives to fill many hours of television prime time? To find out, I was employed not as a researcher but as a story finder. I was faced with over a hundred years' worth of documentation, thousands of original mill records, personal correspondence, thousands of artefacts, no living witnesses and a ticking deadline. I had two weeks.

On my first day I made my first invaluable connection. I met Alkestis Tsilika, Ally. Ally controlled, and still does, the gateway to the archives. She took me to the archive room, where the chill contrasted shockingly with the summer heat outside. Safes were unlocked, *CSI*-type rubber gloves were donned and layer after layer of precious documents were presented in fading cardboard files. I peeled back the first few letters, but what on earth was this? Correspondence in the tiniest of scrawls from the sharpest of quills. Writing crawled across the paper, which had then been turned over and the reverse covered in these hieroglyphics, bleeding through and blurring the already hard-to-read text. Then, in a seeming act of lunacy, the paper had been turned through forty-five degrees and the writing began all over, across and on top of the original text. It was impossibly dense and I felt those two weeks compress into seconds. I began to feel strangely clammy in that chilliest of rooms. I carefully tucked the letters back in their files and peeled off the gloves.

Back in the office and equally carefully, I laid out the enormity of my task and asked Ally if there were people I could talk to, people who'd already attempted to crack these indecipherable codes. After Ally had explained this painfully intricate way of communicating – paper was scarce and expensive, and nobody would waste a square fraction of an inch – she mentioned what would prove to be my next invaluable sources of inspiration and knowledge.

'You should speak to Keith and Ann,' she said. 'They're in on Wednesday . . .'

Quarry Bank Mill archives are regularly pored over by an army of volunteers. Unlike me, they don't give up after a few moments squinting at the scrawling of a seemingly mad person. They persevere. After I'd spent a few minutes talking to Keith

Plant and Ann Rundle, it all began to fall into place for me.

'You should speak to Philip,' they said. Philip Charnley became next on the list. Then Chris Guffogg, and on and on . . .

A lot of speaking to people, then. But what cracked the problem was the listening, and then the looking, in the right places. By the end of that first week I was feeling the history of the mill wash through me, those remarkable lives swimming into vivid focus. And it wasn't just the masters or even the adult workers. To one side of the mill stands the Apprentice House, where the child workers lived, preserved in all its period detail. It took just one scheduled tour to get me hooked. This was a startling insight into life for apprentice children, a life still, surprisingly, little known. As I learned more and more, I thought back to that carefree summer's day, thirty years earlier, when all the day held in store for those free and easy boys was a refreshing, giddy plunge in the river to take their breath away and cleanse them of the sweat and the dust. No such idyll for the children of Quarry Bank Mill.

The stories I unearthed were of course raw material from the pages of history, to be refined by the dramatists as they saw fit. Any television series is going to have to concentrate on a certain, finite number of characters and a certain, finite number of stories. And those characters and stories don't exist in a vacuum; they play out against the wider world. *The Mill* is set at a time of tumultuous change, when wars raged in Europe and America, the cotton industry waxed and waned, fuelled by the horror of slavery, and working-class people struggled to find their voice and push for electoral change and their basic human rights.

As with a lot of dramatic reconstructions of historical events, not all the most dramatically satisfying moments happen at the best, and most convenient, times for the dramatist. In the retelling of these stories it is sometimes for the benefit of the writer and ultimately, therefore, to the benefit of the viewer, that characters and events are slipped from their historically accurate moorings, to a place of greater immediacy and relevance.

In the first series, the core characters are all based on real people, their stories adapted with dramatic licence. At the top of the pecking order are the Greg family: Samuel, the founder of Quarry Bank Mill and its dynasty, his wife Hannah, and one of their sons, Robert Hyde Greg. As in life, the senior Gregs are shown to have had a long and close married life; but the television series has Samuel dying before Hannah. He actually outlived her by some years. There's a powerful dramatic reason for this switch: Samuel represents the old guard, set in his ways; his son Robert Hyde is the thrusting entrepreneur, keen to exploit new technology and strengthen the mill's place in a fiercely competitive industry. Old Samuel has to be out of the way.

The television series is faithful, though, to an important dramatic strand: the Gregs' involvement in the slave trade. Their empire depended on cotton picked by slaves in the southern states of America, and they themselves owned slaves on sugar plantations in Dominica. The real Hannah Greg found this abhorrent; a free-thinking and liberal woman for her time, she held the filthy trade in disdain, associating with other liberals and abolitionists. The television series brings out this continuing tension between husband and wife. Samuel's wealth and position is a constant reminder to Hannah that an evil dwells in the heart of the cotton trade . . .

That wealth and position also depended of course on the labours of the workers, some of whom are also based on real people. Daniel Bate, the clockmaker/mechanic, is shown in the opening episode as being sprung from a debtors' jail by Robert Hyde Greg, who wants to employ Daniel's remarkable technical expertise. The real Daniel was indeed sprung by a Greg, but it actually happened fifty years earlier. It was Robert's father, Samuel Greg, who financed Daniel's freedom and then made sure he paid back the fee to the penny while in his employ. Daniel did marry and settle at the nearby village of Styal, but it wasn't to the pregnant Susannah Catterall. He actually found a bride in the spinning rooms, one Caroline Holland, and left with her the minute he'd paid off his debt to the Gregs. And he wasn't the firebrand of the show. His fictional character reflects the burgeoning political changes in England as working people struggled with the ideology of suffrage and the attainment of individual rights. Hence his association with the political activist John Doherty, another real character but portrayed in his authentic historical period, fighting for the Ten-Hour Bill that would limit children's working hours.

Of all the millworkers, Esther Price stands out. The real Esther encapsulated everything that was bad about life in the mill, and what good there was too. At times, she was both its scourge and its champion. She is winningly portrayed in the series, as a spirited, determined Liverpudlian, and a lot of the things she does are based on reports in the mill memoranda, shown in the stoppages book, documented in the wages ledgers, and further backed up in letters and documents written by the Gregs. Yes, she was placed in isolation with the recently deceased Mrs Timperley, late stewardess of the Apprentice House's girls, but did she ever side with the radical Daniel Bate and try to kickstart a workers' revolution? No. However, I can see why she was chosen for this role. In another time, and with different influences, she may well have done all of those things. She certainly had the will.

An assortment of supporting characters, high and low, are based on real people too. Apprentices like Thomas Priestly, Susanna Catterall (the father of whose baby wasn't actually a Greg), and Esther's old friend and partner in crime, Lucy Garner; the aforementioned Mrs Timperley and her husband, who looked after the boys in the Apprentice House (though at the time of first series, the supervisors were actually Mr and Mrs Shawcross); and the mill's remarkable and historically significant medical man, Dr Holland. Charlie Crout, the apprentice-turned-overlooker, has rather a rough deal. In life he was apparently blameless, but for dramatic purposes he was made to represent the unscrupulous sexual predator, abusing his position to prey on the young female workers – a phenomenon all too common at the time.

In the first televised series screenwriter John Fay skilfully plundered the research material and brought the stories and characters thrillingly to life, creating a compelling drama, true to the real people and historical events. The series was aired in July

2013 and was a hit, striking a chord with many viewers for its unflinching and evidently authentic portrayal of mill life. A second series was commissioned, and again it drew on those priceless records. New characters were introduced and added new dimensions. The Howlett family especially, arriving from rural Buckinghamshire where they'd endured the direst poverty, forced to travel to find work, any work, that would keep them alive. John Howlett was a proud agricultural labourer, wanting to work for his money rather than falling back on the charity of the hated workhouse. In the series he takes up arms against his fellow workers; this is not documented, but of a piece with his determination to earn an honest wage, whatever the circumstances and conditions.

While Howlett undoubtedly existed, there is no evidence that anyone resembling Peter, the Dominican ex-plantation slave featured in the second series, ever appeared in Styal. However, he offers us a graphic slice of the horror suffered in Dominica by those who worked in the Greg plantations, and his back story is based on a real incident. He is both a powerful character and a metaphor for this struggle, representing the shameful slaving past (and present) of the family.

Six months after the first series debuted, I had another call from Emily Dalton, only this time with the chill of Christmas in the air. Would I like to write a book about Quarry Bank Mill, to accompany the series? It took a heartbeat to say yes.

Fortunately for me, I could call again on Ally and her band of volunteers – Keith, Ann, Philip – and employees like Chris, as enthusiastic and helpful as ever. For this undertaking far outweighed the original task I'd been given. I plunged once more into the massive archives, finding new data all the time: the letters, the diaries, the public declarations, the historical texts, the pamphlets, the photographs . . . One of the great pleasures for me was the many conversations I had with all those knowledgeable people. It's all there if you know where to look and if you ask the right guides. And beyond the archives I found several vital books on the subject, particularly David Sekers's definitive account of Hannah Greg's life, *A Lady of Cotton*.

Quarry Bank Mill and Styal offer arguably the most intact colonies of historical and industrial significance in Europe. Their combined histories offer us a microcosm of one of the most turbulent periods ever known in this country, and one that can be traced to the present in the forms of descendants of the apprentice children, still living in the village today. And it's not even as though it's all locked away, sitting in aspic. Anyone can visit and see for themselves; anyone can stand in those rooms and absorb the very history of the place. As I have.

In this book I aim to do what the television series have done: breathe life into those old documents and bring the children, the mill and the village into sharp focus. Not just the life and times of characters featured on television, but those before, during and after them. This will of course call for degrees of speculation, but informed speculation. For, after all, isn't all history based on the passing-down of stories, the accurate interpretation of any given event and any given life, the interpretation of documents? I have been able to tease the personal details out of the vast archive at the mill, to ask the questions that hadn't been previously asked, to make connections not previously made.

We'll be looking at the human side of an industrial empire, the challenges and power struggles facing Samuel and his heirs, and the struggles of organised labour to make itself heard. But above all we'll witness the lives of the children, as they found themselves thrust breathlessly into the riotous, dangerous daily grind of a millworker, expected to learn quickly or find themselves maimed, dead, or back in the workhouse where most of them came from. And yet, out of this misery, are tales of lives lived to the full, as far as was possible in the circumstances. Examples of the triumph of the indomitable human spirit; born not necessarily out of heroism and resistance, but out of the basic need to survive. When backed into corners, some people are cowed into a paltry existence, while others seek, and find, solace in the small victories over their lot. Some even soar and rise triumphantly above their humble beginnings.

This story has them all.

Acknowledgements

In the course of writing this book, I have sought the aid of many, many people who have shared their expertise and knowledge willingly and often joyfully. They are, sadly, too numerous to mention and I apologise in advance if their names do not appear on this page. There are those whose contributions I cannot omit for the very reason that this book would not have been written without them. Emily Dalton, for her belief in The Mill and her belief in me. Emma Tait for her unfailing enthusiasm and instinct and Christine King for her doggedness and sheer hard work. Immense thanks to all those toiling in the Quarry Bank archives and especially Ally, their guardian and someone, who with the crook of an eyebrow, can tell you not only how far wide of the mark you may be, but how far she may be prepared to let you go. All the staff at Quarry Bank Mill too, who have made me feel part of the team there, under the marvellous guidance of Eleanor Underhill. To say I was inspired by Ann Rundle and Keith Plant is to massively understate the case, one afternoon in their presence was enough for me to realise that this book was not only possible but that it had to be written. My thanks to David Sekers, for the kind permissions granted to me in quoting from his book. Finally my wife, Anne, and family, mad, bad and fabulous to know, but a constant source of joy and inspiration.

DH May 2014

CHAPTER ONE

Foundations

I'm standing in the middle of the mill meadow, the ideal vantage point to take in the whole valley. Families picnic on tartan blankets as children chase one another through shin-high grass and dandelion clocks. Their yelps of delight are the only sounds to pierce the calm that settles on the valley under the suffocating August sun. I've been retracing my steps of thirty years ago, that summer's walk along the River Bollin. I think of Samuel Greg first coming across this land, and straightaway seeing its possibilities. Chances are he would have stood where I stand, listening to the river gurgling by, twisting his head to survey the panoramic theatre presented by the high-sided valley and the trees lining the cliffs. He would have been assessing, dreaming and planning. He knew he wanted to build his mill on a river, but he also knew that the Bollin might need a helping hand if it was to power the sort of waterwheel he had in mind. Weirs, lakes, sluices, tunnels . . . a complex web of mechanics and engineering probably started to weave in his mind. Therefore, he knew he needed help himself, specialists to make his dream come true. I stand here merely marvelling at his creation, clutching my guide book and sporting the sticker that gives me access all areas.

I fan the pages of the guide book, and suddenly notice a detail in one of the captions. Doing a quick sum in my head, I think back to a week ago when I was going through my own, personal archives for a family celebration. I'd dug out a grainy three-by-five print of a young man leaning proprietorially across the roof of an ancient Peugeot. He has a Viking's beard, shoulder-length hair and improbably flared jeans. He's me, aged twenty-two – that same young man who had decided not to waste an idyllic summer's day in an old mill. I realise now that Samuel Greg was twenty-two when he built his first mill. Twenty-two! In my twenty-second summer I was aimless, drifting and unfocused, wearing some pretty bad jeans. Samuel was on the cusp of creating a dynasty within the spinning and weaving business community that would help Manchester become the envy of the industrial world. At the very least, I can try to do justice to the history he created, and the life stories he helped forge; uncover the secrets behind the forbidding mill walls, and peer into its darkest corners for traces of the lives of those apprenticed children who gave up their innocence and youth to fuel the industrial fires of the devouring cotton trade.

Samuel is an old man when the television drama opens – nearly fifty years have passed since he built the mill, in 1784. He's supposed to be retired, allowing his son Robert Hyde Greg to control the business. But Samuel can't bear to let go of his beloved mill, his first success. His ears are attuned to every beat of the mill's mechanical heart, and any skipping hastens him from Hannah's side and on to the mill's floors. As Robert Hyde pushes for modernisation, Samuel becomes like a stag at bay, knowing his days are numbered but still proudly up for the fight.

His father, Thomas Greg, originally from Scotland but living in Ireland, had built up a successful many-faceted empire, sourcing his raw material from slave plantations in the American South, and building up wealth from sugar produced in his own slave plantations in Dominica. Thomas had another string to his bow, in the form of privateering in the Atlantic – in other words, piracy and smuggling. In 1770s Belfast the economic situation was precarious, and Thomas sent his two eldest sons to England to build careers for themselves. One son was Samuel, only eight years old; his brother, Thomas Jnr, was sixteen. Once in England, Thomas was to go his own way, eventually carving a successful career in insurance and establishing a country residence at Coles, Hertfordshire. Young Samuel took lodgings with his mother's brothers, Robert and Nathaniel Hyde, to learn his way around their trade as merchants and manufacturers of linen and fustian, a rough cloth.

The Hyde brothers were a mixed blessing for Samuel. While the childless Robert favoured him, making him his heir, Nathaniel, a renowned drunkard and gambler, was jealous, trying to steer Samuel away from the business – even suggesting that he should be a parson. Nathaniel himself had no male heir, he and his wife having produced only daughters. After Robert's death, Nathaniel gave up the business and sold his stock to Samuel, on the proviso that he, Nathaniel, never fathered a boy. This stock was sold in a market depressed by the war with the American colonies and Samuel got it for a good price. Then a series of crucial events followed: the war ended and Samuel's stock soared, making him a huge profit of £14,000. Nathaniel died, leaving a pregnant wife. She then gave birth to a boy, too late for him to inherit immediately; Samuel remained the boy's guardian until he was old enough to share in the inheritance.

Meanwhile, as well as this generous inheritance, he had the goodwill and contacts of the Hyde business, and wide-ranging experience in the rapidly expanding Manchester cotton trade. Samuel was in a good position to establish his own industrialised spinning mill, and cast about for a suitable site. At that time, before the use of steam engines, waterwheels provided the power to work the machinery, so he needed a fast-flowing river. Hence his arrival on the banks of the Bollin. Samuel decided to call his first mill Quarry Bank. An empire was born.

As long as Samuel ran the mill, it was exclusively for spinning; his weavers worked traditionally, in their own village homes, using hand looms. His early millworkers were recruited locally, most walking to the mill from surrounding areas such as Wilmslow, Handforth and Morley. It was only when the mill grew in production that Samuel had to look further afield and began the process of taking on apprentices and, in many cases, whole families. This meant housing them, and slowly but surely the outbuildings of Oak Farm at nearby Styal were converted for his workforce. These weren't apprentices in the modern sense; these children were indentured for a set time, usually until they were eighteen, and then set to work, unpaid, doing the most menial, yet dangerous, tasks. In essence they belonged to the Gregs and the mill until adulthood or death claimed them.

Nearly all of them were orphans, from the workhouse, the only 'home' available to paupers. There were limits to how far away they could be taken from their home parish, usually a 40-mile radius (though for the young children it might as well have been as far as the Moon). Initially, the Newcastle-under-Lyme workhouse supplied Samuel's apprentices, then, when the supply there dried up, the focus shifted to the Liverpool Workhouse, which features significantly in the television series when Esther flees the mill and returns to her home town of Liverpool, hoping to find the evidence she needs to prove her real age. Samuel eventually built the Apprentice House for his growing army of child workers in 1790.

Why this dependence on child labour? Children were cheap, of course, receiving bed and board in lieu of wages. But what made them indispensable was, quite simply, their size and their nimble fingers. Only they were small enough to dart under, through and round the moving machinery, picking up loose cotton and other rubbish that could otherwise cause jams or – most dreaded of all in tinderbox conditions – fire. It was self-evidently a most hazardous job, and indeed casualties were common, yet the supply of children was inexhaustible. Lose one, and there'll be another along in a minute. Grinding poverty made sure of that.

The advent of the Industrial Revolution from the mid-1770s added another dimension to the suffering of the poor. It was the painful transition of an economy based on working by hand to one based on increasingly sophisticated, powered machinery, concentrating workers in grim factories, subjecting them to a twilight world of unremitting toil, unavoidable ill-health, and frequently premature death. A dark and satanic life indeed.

Traditionally, poor men without a trade had worked in agriculture. These agricultural labourers and their families relied on the steady supply of work on the land closest to them. If this dried up, they became itinerant, forever shifting in search of work, families in tow. However, by the time Samuel Greg stood back and admired the laying of the first brick on his brand-new mill at Styal, working the land was becoming less and less viable for many of these 'ag labs'.

We can trace the decline in this trade back to the sixteenth century, when the price of grain was comparatively low set against that of wool. For the landowners, the thinking was simple: why keep high-maintenance arable land when you could turn it over to sheep farming, with acre after acre looked over by one man and a dog? Just clear out the old labourers. At the same time, the wholesale land-grabbing that resulted from the dissolution of the monasteries under King Henry VIII made the situation worse. Landowners, already wealthy and with not an altruistic bone in their bodies, gobbled up these monastery estates, increasing rents and stuffing their quickly deepening pockets. Things could have changed more than a century later during the Civil War of 1642–51, but what emerged was a greater distance between the haves and the have-nots. Slowly but surely, aristocratic landowners sucked up power and money. As peers, they had their say in the House of Lords, while they gained control of the House of Commons and, through patronage, increased their influence in the Church. As justices of the peace, they became responsible for local government and inexorably became law-makers. By the eighteenth century, the seamless rise of the ruling classes was unstoppable, and they could instigate the system of Enclosure that consolidated their power – an early example of privatisation of public assets. What had traditionally been common land, like open fields, available to common people, was 'enclosed', creating individual plots of land that were privately owned.

Eventually the landowners, a tiny proportion of the population, enclosed 14 million acres of common land. Farmers and ag labs working the land could stay on as tenants, but paying ever higher rents. These extortionate rents were supposedly to encourage a better standard of farming and general land use, but more usually they simply drove out smaller concerns, forcing farmers to migrate or become landless labourers. This resulted in thousands of dispossessed poor people wandering aimlessly in a desperate search for work and food. Families at the end of their endurance were forced into workhouses, administered by parsimonious parish officials and infamous for their cruel, harsh conditions. (After all, you wouldn't want workhouses to be places where people actually wanted to stay . . .) In the most desperate circumstances, parents had to surrender their children to the untender mercies of the workhouse while they themselves went further afield looking for work. Or, of course, they'd simply die, leaving helpless orphans. When whole communities fell on hard times, the workhouses were full to overflowing with desolate human beings.

Samuel Greg was one of many millowners who, with business booming, sought to expand their workforce with displaced ag labs. In part, his hand was forced by the remote location of Quarry Bank – ag labs were all he could get. Most of them were only used to working outdoors and the degree of freedom this allowed. They weren't used to the rules and stringent timekeeping demanded by a disciplined work regime. The weather and seasons dictated their lives and timetables, not the overlookers or the mill managers. So they usually made poor millhands, especially the men, being intransigent and unruly – we'll be looking at them again in the next chapter. Meanwhile, there were always the children.

With the sweated labour of his workers, and his own energy and determination, Samuel was beginning to make his mill a flourishing concern. As a gentleman of substance, with a high standing in the cotton community, all he needed now was a wife. And it was his choice of wife that was to set the ethos of Quarry Bank Mill, and have an enormous effect on both the business and the dynasty – and on the lives of child apprentices.

Hannah Lightbody was chalk to Samuel Greg's cheese, he a dashing, forthright Irish businessman and she a principled, high-minded daughter of a Unitarian merchant from relatively liberal Liverpool. Was she ready for someone like Samuel? Certainly she had little time for her contemporaries, writing, 'what a troop of shallow brained fellows the young men of Liverpool are'. She associated with many prominent philanthropists and abolitionists, who were passionate opponents of the slave trade. After what seems, from letters in the archives, to be a difficult courtship (of which more later), Hannah and Samuel married in 1789, setting up home in Manchester. Quite apart from her estimable qualities, Hannah brought a very useful dowry to the marriage. Ambitious Samuel used her £10,000 to expand the mill at Quarry Bank, ordering the construction of the largest waterwheel in Europe to drive his thousands of spindles.

Hannah abhorred life in the cluttered, filthy centre of Manchester. She pined for the rather more elevated society of Liverpool, and found respite only in the rural retreat in Styal where she and the children could take holidays. After more than ten years of what was sometimes a troubled, joyless (for her part) marriage, in 1800 she was delighted when Samuel built a family home, Quarry Bank House. Anything to escape Manchester with its grime and its danger. What better place than the very valley she had spent many a happy time with her children? Even though there was the huge chunk of compromise in the shape of the adjacent mill.

By 1808, Hannah and Samuel had ten surviving children, five boys and five girls. Hannah was a great champion of children's education, even for girls, who generally lost out in this patriarchal society. Her enlightened views, along with the new proximity to the workplace, led her to take a keen interest in the workers as a whole, and especially in the youngest and most vulnerable, the child apprentices. She saw to it that they lived in reasonably decent conditions (for the time), ate nourishing if plain food, had due medical attention, and received a basic education. (At least, the boys were taught to read and write; girls were confined to sewing – maybe Hannah wasn't altogether consistent here.) She looked after their spiritual wellbeing too, making sure they attended church on Sundays. This level of care was just about unheard-of. Naturally, you wanted the most from your workers, so you made sure they had the bare minimum to keep them alive and making money for you. Hannah would have been more than painfully aware of her husband's ties with slavery, and perhaps this fuelled her altruism when it came to her very own version of slaves?

Hannah also had her Dissenter religion and background. Dissenters were always a thorn in the side of the established Church, being free-thinking, radical and tolerant. Hannah's Unitarianism was a relatively new sect, which denied the Holy Trinity, proclaiming God as a single entity and Jesus Christ to be a mortal man, the flesh-and-blood son of Mary and Joseph. This was heresy. Dissenters generally came under such suspicion that they were barred from attending the universities of the time and couldn't take up political office. It's no coincidence that many successful business entrepreneurs came from the ranks of Dissenters; free thinkers with fewer limits to their ambitions. Hannah, being a woman and therefore unfit for business, channelled her dissenting fervour into the welfare of others. It may well be that Samuel too had some empathy with the child workers. He wouldn't have forgotten that he himself was once an apprentice, sent away from home and family at a tender age to live and work in a strange land. He certainly took pleasure in rewarding good work, touring the factory floors to dole out alms. He was in the habit of leaving a sixpence (six hours' overtime!) on the machine of a particularly diligent worker. Once it was rumoured that he left three of them on the same machine. He and Hannah also held prize-giving evenings at the house, where the best workers of any year were awarded gifts for their efforts. In short, the whole Greg family were renowned for, and prided themselves on, their humane treatment of their workers.

Well, humane up to a point. By modern standards, cushioned and conditioned by Health and Safety, working conditions were simply horrendous. It's just that other mills were a great deal worse, as we shall see. Anyway, Samuel Greg was too hard-nosed a businessman to let sentiment get in the way of a profit. When the poorest parishes asked him to take apprentice children off their hands he charged them up to £4, rather than the usual £2. He also insisted they came with smocks and other clothing, and had to pass a medical and a trial period. He may have been influenced by Hannah, but he wasn't a soft touch. Business was business. He was always dead set against the Ten-Hour Bill, maintaining it would be a disaster in such a competitive business to reduce working hours for children. His influence here lived on after his death: when Parliament finally passed the bill, in 1847, Quarry Bank – and the other mills that Samuel had later built – flouted the law and carried on regardless for years, often being fined for doing so.

Samuel had built those mills, in Lancaster, Caton, Bollington and Bury, in order to provide a business for each of his sons. The eldest, Thomas Tylston, didn't enter the cotton trade at all, having been named by Samuel's older brother, Thomas of Coles, as his heir. Young Thomas went off to Coles and lived the life of a wealthy gentleman. Of his four brothers, Robert Hyde was to inherit Quarry Bank. The next son, John, took over the mills in Lancaster and Caton, while Samuel Jnr was destined for Bollington. The youngest son, William Rathbone (who was not the father of Susannah's Catterall's baby!), took over the Bury Mill. These scions were to have mixed success. The rounded, liberal education secured for them by their loving mother wasn't necessarily the best preparation for a cut-throat business world . . .

The tension between Samuel Snr and Robert Hyde is brought out in the first television series by Samuel refusing to introduce weaving machines to Quarry Bank, despite his son's pleas. In reality Samuel held sway over Robert Hyde and Quarry Bank for too long, only relinquishing control after an accident in the grounds. The old stag was attacked by a startled deer and never fully recovered, writing to Robert Hyde, 'I feel my powers of body and mind rapidly in decay . . .' Only after Samuel's death in 1834 could Robert Hyde have his own way. By this time the real Hannah had been dead for six years, and no doubt her soothing, conciliatory presence was missed.

* * *

Quarry Bank Mill was to continue working for over a century, under successive Gregs, until 1959, by which time it was in the care of the National Trust. The Greg dynasty was well and truly over, but the lives of those who kept the mill turning are now held up to the light: their histories, their daily routine, their pains and small pleasures – their endurance and their survival.

CHAPTER TWO

Leaving Home

'Home' for child apprentices was never going to be the cosy domestic hearth, in the care of loving parents. As we've seen, their last stop before the mill was usually the workhouse. And for most people the workhouse was absolutely the last resort, when all else had failed. Such were the values of the time that poor people were considered sinful, responsible for their own poverty, and only punitive treatment would force them to get on the straight and narrow (and stop them being a charge on the parish). So life in the workhouse was nasty, brutal and inevitably short. Inmates lived in squalid, cramped conditions, with poor sanitation and abysmal food, often sleeping three or more to a rudimentary cot. And they had no rights: if overseers were vile and brutal, or sexually abusive, there was no redress. If the guardians appointed to supervise the workhouse turned a blind eye to abuse, then for the inmates it was more like living in a penal settlement than a place of refuge.

As if these routine threats weren't enough, there was always the danger of sudden catastrophe. Fire was as dreaded in the workhouse as in the cotton mill. In another time, Esther Price and her friend Lucy Garner might have been among the pitiful casualties of a devastating tragedy at Liverpool Workhouse. On 8 September 1862, a schoolmistress there, Miss Kennan, raised the alarm around two o'clock in the morning. Dense smoke was pouring from the children's dormitory. Water pressure was too low for fire hoses to do any good, and access was difficult with doors at the ends of the dorms. The staff strove frantically to get everyone out but, faced with an inferno, had to back down knowing they'd left children inside. The following morning revealed the scale of their efforts and the dismal sight of those who perished. The roof and part of the dorm floor had gone, and masonry was scattered everywhere. Several bodies were discovered among the debris around the beds, some crushed, all burned beyond recognition. By far the saddest sight was that of fourteen iron beds still lined along one of the walls. In a grotesque parody of the sanctity of children tucked up safely at night, there lay the charred remains of fourteen children who had never even managed to get out of bed. All told, the fire claimed twenty-one children, all aged between four and seven, and two of their nurses.

Liverpool Workhouse was already notorious, for a quite different reason. In 1843, ten years after Esther and Lucy left, it was recorded by stipendiary magistrate Mr Rushton that supervision had become somewhat 'lax' at the workhouse and that widespread prostitution had become the norm. In some parts, 'abandoned profligates' were living next to ordinary folk and access could be achieved between the male and female sections over a wall by removing the broken glass from its top.

Women 'wearing only shifts' were going over and servicing the men on the other side and relieving them of any scant amount of money they'd managed to squirrel away. Parts of the building had become areas where the governor feared to tread. Mr Rushton concluded that the Liverpool Workhouse had become 'the largest brothel in England'. Children ending up there found themselves trying to survive in a place where society had broken down and fear and death stalked the corridors. When the fictional Esther flees Quarry Bank to go back to Liverpool, she too is forced to sell herself in return for sanctuary and to keep alive her hopes of finding out her real age. In these hard times, sexuality was a common currency.

Half a century later, Liverpool could boast another dubious title, that of the largest workhouse in Britain, demonstrating the growing tidal wave of poverty and deprivation. By 1893, it was housing over 3,000 inmates. There was some medical care, an innovation of leading philanthropist William Rathbone some thirty years earlier. Even so, inmates were dying at the rate of twenty per week.

At least Liverpool didn't feature in one of the worst workhouse abuses ever known in this country. It happened in 1845, in Andover. Author Peter Higginbotham, an authority on workhouse life in Victorian times, gives a vivid account of a very murky scandal, showing just what depths people could sink to if they were helpless. Inmates were routinely forced to work at the most unpleasant jobs that other people wouldn't touch, like bone-crushing. Here, the bones of horses, dogs and other animals were pounded into a powder used for fertiliser a back-breaking and dangerous procedure, using a 28lb length of solid iron. What made things worse for the Andover inmates was that their master, a corrupt and venal man, was systematically stealing their rations. Through the investigations of a radical MP, Thomas Wakley, it eventually came out that starving bone-crushers were scavenging any shreds of meat left. In the words of one inmate, 61-year-old Samuel Green:

> I was employed in the workhouse at bone-breaking the best part of my time . . . We looked out for the fresh bones; we used to tell the fresh bones by the look of them, and then we used to be like a parcel of dogs after them; some were not so particular about the bones being fresh as others; I like fresh bones; I never touched one that was a little high; the marrow was as good as the meat, it was all covered over by bone, and no filth could get to it . . . I have picked a sheep's head, a mutton bone and a beef bone; that was when they were fresh and good; sometimes I have had one that was stale and stunk, and I eat it even then; I eat it when it was stale and stinking because I was hungered . . .

The outrage sent shivers through the whole country and led to reforms. Bone-breaking was outlawed, and the Poor Law Commissioners were replaced in 1847 by a new Poor Law Board, more accountable to Parliament. And of course the old workhouse master was sacked. Was his replacement any better? He was three years into his tenure when he was dismissed for 'taking liberties with female paupers'. And also, it transpired, was his son.

Terrible conditions, ever-present danger from abuse, disease, starvation and sudden death . . . you'd imagine that inmates would be as ready to leave the workhouse as they'd been reluctant to enter it. Indeed, they would jump at the chance, if they'd been led to believe that even a marginally better life awaited them outside. At least, the children did, not knowing any better.

It wasn't uncommon for unsuspecting children to be bamboozled by parish officials keen to offload them and by unscrupulous agents trawling for recruits. The life of Robert Blincoe is a good illustration of this. He described his early years to a journalist from Bolton, John Brown, who wrote it up in *The Memoirs of Robert Blincoe* in 1822. Robert, incarcerated in St Pancras Workhouse, London, was that most pitiable and vulnerable of paupers, a foundling. He never knew his parents and, to his anguish when he realised, the workhouse had kept no records of them.

Mothers died in childbirth, or later from disease or accident. Working fathers often suffered early deaths, especially in the mills. Many children found themselves in the workhouse with no memories of their parents, or just a vague recollection. They were utterly alone. Other workhouse children could hope to be reclaimed by parents, given a change of fortune, but the orphaned would never be able to harbour such dreams of being saved, being reunited with loved ones. Their only family was to be found in the workhouse, their peers, and the wardens of the workhouse – adults they trusted wholeheartedly. So when the very people they had grown to trust regaled them with tales of what could be achieved living the life of a millhand, how could they resist?

The children in Robert's workhouse heard of an impending visit from representatives of a Nottingham mill, and the stewards stoked their already fevered imaginations:

> Prior to the show-day of the pauper children to the purveyor or cotton master, the most illusive and artfully contrived false-hoods were spread, to fill the minds of those poor infants with the most absurd and ridiculous errors, as to the real nature of the servitude, to which they were to be consigned. It was gravely stated to them, according to Blincoe's statement, made in the most positive and solemn manner, that they were all, when they arrived at the cotton mill, to be transformed into ladies and gentlemen: that they would be fed on roast beef and plum-puddings, be allowed to ride their master's horses and have silver watches, and plenty of cash in their pockets. Nor was it the nurses, or other inferior persons of the workhouse, with whom this vile deception originated, but with the parish officers themselves.

The heavily burdened parishes gave up their wards readily. It was too expensive to keep feeding the number of children they housed – far better to pay the likes of Samuel Greg and see them off with false promises of a better way of life. Of course, this deception was realised only when it was too late and the children were harnessed to the mills and their infernal machines. Did the parish officers and stewards of the workhouses know the scope of their own falsehood? Perhaps the millowners themselves fed these lies to gullible parishes who were far too ready to believe them?

In a telling, if fictional, story in the first television series, we see the Apprentice House steward, Mr Timperley, collecting two young girls from the Liverpool Workhouse, Lucy and Catherine Garner. He smoothly assures the official that frail little Catherine will flourish: 'She needs feeding up and looking after – that's what we do at Quarry Mill.' Maybe that would be enough to allay any lingering parish doubts. Timperley then, taking the girls to the mill in his cart, tells them to breathe in the good clean country air. 'Cough all the city shit out of your lungs,' he says. Yes, we think, and replace it with another kind, the kind that will actually rob you of your very breath. His treacherous behaviour reaches a heartbreaking low when he's taking Catherine back to the workhouse, after she's been rejected as unfit by the mill. Timperley, all avuncular kindness, tells her the people in the workhouse will be vexed with her, so he'll let her escape. He points in the opposite direction from Liverpool, across a desolate and bitterly cold landscape, assuring her that there's a town full of good people who'll look after her. The little girl reluctantly climbs down from the cart and stumbles off, clutching her pathetic bundle. The next time we see Catherine it is as a wind-blown mound of rags and bones in a featureless field. Timperley keeps the money he should have given back to the workhouse, and stuffs himself with steak and ale, putting in a receipt for it all against expenses. The real Timperley may well have been subsequently judged 'unfit' for the purpose of running the Apprentice House, but he was no monster.

The truth behind real-life deceptions didn't emerge until apprentices began to escape the mills and tell their stories, like Robert Blincoe and our own Esther Price and Thomas Priestly, and until the likes of John Doherty published his crusading pamphlets (such as his reprint of Robert Blincoe's memoirs in 1832).

Another kind of deception involved children's ages. It was a common occurrence for workhouse children to arrive not knowing their age, and agreeing to whatever their new masters wrote down. Children were indentured to work as apprentices till the age of eighteen (though in the television series, it's twenty-one for Esther). Future employers would get more work out of them if their ages were dropped by a year or two. In the case of Esther, her real age was dropped by three years. Her indenture, signed by one John Park, overseer of the poor of Liverpool, is dated 14 November 1833. Her age at this time was entered as being eleven years old. This, as it transpired, was simply not true, and Esther knew it – not that her protestations would get her anywhere, once it was down in writing.

Esther had been born to Thomas and Maria Price, in Harrison Street, Liverpool. Thomas was a sailmaker, albeit clearly not a successful one. Baptismal records in the registers of St Peter's, Liverpool, show the full family: two brothers, Richard and John, and two sisters, Margaret and Martha, as well as Esther. Just why Esther was apparently the only one to be sent to the workhouse isn't known. Maybe she was just one mouth too many to feed. Or perhaps she was the biggest mouth, a real pain for her family. We don't know. At least her older sister Martha was prepared to help Esther later on, when the issue of her real age was raised. Martha appears in the television drama doing just this, and then makes a later, more sorrowful but entirely fictional, appearance in the second series, having fallen on hard times herself.

Although most apprentice children came from the workhouse, there were exceptions. Parents could die at any time, suddenly leaving their children bereft of care and money. Poverty was no respecter of class or social standing; this is how the Chelsea girls ended up at Quarry Bank. Eleven of them are recorded as being moved to Styal from the Royal Military Asylum at Chelsea, where the orphaned children of soldiers were given refuge. As we saw in the last chapter, there were limits to how far apprentices could be moved from the parish looking after them. London also had a 40-mile rule, but it seems this could be overridden in some circumstances.

Having a soldier for a father conferred a degree of social status, and life for their children in the barracks at Chelsea would have provided security and a kind of stability. But of course there was an increased risk of early death. When fathers were killed in action, their children's world was tipped upside-down, the fall sudden and shocking. Bereaved families were moved into the asylum, where they would be safe. The best outlook would be for the widowed mother to marry again, but unfortunately there was a dearth of available men and too many widowed women. Sadly, on occasion, the mother died first, leaving the children alone in the asylum while their father was away soldiering. In this case, the children might be able to stay there, or they might not. The worst fate would be to lose the surviving parent, in which case the child would be an orphan and an instant burden.

When, in 1815, Samuel Greg heard that the asylum wanted to offload these girls, he stepped into this particular breach. Quarry Bank archivist Keith Plant has tracked the Chelsea girls down and, as ever, with his simply stated factual files, drawing on the Royal Military Asylum records, each tells a heartbreaking story.

The first batch of girls had much in common. Margaret (Peggy) Curley was born in 1801, and admitted to the asylum when she was seven. Her father is shown as Private Michael Curley of the 335th Foot regiment, later of the Suffolk Regiment. Her mother, Mary, is accorded one note that simply reads 'deceased'. Seven years later, on 9 April 1815, another entry, for Peggy, reads 'discharged'. At some time in between these dates, Peggy would have been sat down by her father while he explained that he would be leaving to serve in the Suffolk Regiment and that she couldn't follow him. On the melancholy day of her departure, Peggy's only comfort would have been that she didn't make the long journey to the unknown north alone. Sharing the carriage north to Quarry Bank were three other girls.

Jane McMillan was the same age as Peggy and had been admitted to the asylum in 1809. Her father was Private James McMillan of 391st Regiment, later serving with the 91st Regiment. Jane's mother is also simply entered as being 'deceased'. Not even a name. So, another father–daughter chat, another discharge notice in the ledger. Elizabeth Sullivan was the same age too, though she had been admitted to the asylum in 1805, when she was four. Her mother, another Mary, is entered only as being 'deceased'. Her father, Private David Sullivan, served in the 287th Foot Regiment until 1815, when he switched to the Prince of Wales Own Irish Regiment. Whether this move or his death precipitated Elizabeth's removal from the asylum is unknown, but move she did.

Making up that quartet of girls from Chelsea was Mary Reilly, a year younger than the other girls. She was admitted to the asylum on 30 August 1806, presumably on the death of her mother, who also remains unnamed. Her father, Private Garret Reilly of the 160th Foot Regiment, moved regiments in 1815 when Mary was thirteen years old. To survive those nine long years with only the memory of her mother and a mostly absent father must have been an ordeal for Mary, and she would know that a move to another regiment could mean she had to leave the asylum. What exactly happened next is unknown. What is known is that alongside the entry for Garret Reilly is the word 'deceased'.

Did Mary wave goodbye to her father before she was

shipped out with Jane, Peggy and Elizabeth? Or did she have that dreaded official visit from an asylum steward, bearing the most awful of news? Which would be worse – leaving the safety of the asylum knowing your father had to give you up, then learning of his death later that year; or to hear of his death, knowing for certain that this terrible news would also mean the end of your time in Chelsea?

The girls would probably have drawn strength and solidarity from their common background. I can imagine them banding together when confronted with the array of Scousers, Potters and Mancs awaiting them at Quarry Bank. Each Chelsea girl knew full well that there was no one coming to retrieve them from their home, so far away, further even than the displaced Liverpool girls. They weren't to be alone for long, though. In September of that same year, their ranks were swelled by half a dozen more girls from Chelsea – they must have made up a formidable clique at Quarry Bank. Again, these new girls were all much of an age, with similar backgrounds. One of them, Margaret Hussey, had a younger sister, Elizabeth, who was later to join her at Styal. Unusually, the Hussey parents were still alive when each of their daughters left; we can only speculate why they couldn't hold on to them: yet another variation on fractured families. At least by the time Elizabeth arrived, at the age of fourteen, Margaret would have been a veteran of the mill rooms and a comforting presence for her.

The youngest of all the Chelsea girls, Elizabeth McGinn, had possibly been in more need of comfort than most when she was admitted to the asylum in 1805. She was just three years and three months old when her mother died. When her father had to change regiments after Waterloo, it was time for Elizabeth to make the long journey north. Such sad beginnings, yet Elizabeth, as we shall see later, was one of those child apprentices who, against the odds, fought hard to try and make a good life for themselves. Another intriguing piece of evidence concerning the Chelsea girls remains in the Manchester Central Library, a letter to Samuel Greg from the authorities at Chelsea, circa 1823.

> Letter to Samuel Greg from Lt Colonel, Royal Military Asylum Chelsea.
>
> Mr Greg is requested to return the enclosed indentures when agreed to Lt Colonel Williamson, Commandant, Royal Military Asylum Chelsea and in order to save the heavy expense of postage will be pleased to put them under one envelope addressed to the Rt Honorable, the Secretary of War, War Office, London.

Where the destinies and cares of children were concerned, cost, as ever, was of prime concern. We will do what we can, but we will always watch the pennies.

So far, we've seen apprentice children leaving whatever home they had as orphans, or as good as. But there were others, with one or more parent surviving, who were still living together as part of a family, which tragically had to be torn apart. The three Bowden sisters, Sarah, Mary and Hannah, who were at Quarry Bank at the same time as Esther Price, suffered this fate.

Jonas Bowden, a labourer, lived with his wife and four children in nearby Mobberley. When his wife died in 1830, Sarah was nine, Mary seven, and Hannah five. They had a younger brother, Thomas. Now Jonas was faced with the awful dilemma of a single parent: how to keep working to put food on the table and yet still look after his children. Many men in his situation would have rapidly remarried, if only to provide a mother for their children. Jonas didn't, and for four years after the death of his wife he tried desperately to cope. Until he couldn't, and made the heartbreaking decision to turn his daughters over to the Gregs. At least he managed to hold on to Thomas.

So near, yet so far from their true home. Was this pain of separation worse for the Bowden sisters than for other apprentices whose surviving family members were living further afield, like a few of the Chelsea girls? On Sundays, when the apprentices were paraded up to the church of St Bart's in Wilmslow, I wonder if the sisters would have searched frantically for a sight of Jonas or Thomas on the way.

Some parents may have made the promise to come back one day and retrieve their children, but these promises were seldom kept. Some children and their parents actually believed that the mills were a place of opportunity – we've seen how easily people could be duped. Modern parents would find the very thought of giving up their child into any sort of labour, and dangerous labour at that, anathema. Parents in earlier centuries didn't have the luxury of choice (and of course there are still sweat shops around the world, and every kind of child exploitation . . .)

Other parents had any choice taken from them. Catherine Sullivan was sent by the Liverpool Overseers for the Poor to Quarry Bank in 1828. Her age was noted as eleven years. She was indentured to serve for seven years, taking her up to eighteen. Then a curious note appeared on her indenture, dated 21 January 1832. And, with this note, Catherine's secret. It seems that Catherine was not a native of Liverpool after all. She must have spoken with a broad Manchester accent, because it was revealed that she'd come from Bradford, north of Manchester. How had she ended up in the Liverpool Workhouse? Catherine had run away from her Bradford home some time around 1828. The note was applied because her parents had tracked her down a full four years after she'd fled and had come to take her home. How must they have felt during this time, to lose an eleven-year-old girl and get her back at fifteen? The stories she must have had to tell, the flight from home, the trip to Liverpool, the despicable workhouse, the terror of working in the mill. Did Catherine ever spend any time regretting her decisions? Surely there must have been many shivering nights when she cried out for her parents to find her, only to be told to shut it by those desperate for the balm of sleep. Catherine was fortunate: she was reclaimed.

There's yet another family permutation leading to the mill, when they would all migrate together as a unit. Keith Plant, champion of the apprentices, has unearthed a touching story that gets to the heart of what was happening in this country as the cotton industry expanded and demanded a never-ending supply of labour (until the next slump). We've already seen the involvement of displaced and desperate agricultural labourers. This story goes back to the beginning, when a letter dated 4 December 1834 was sent to the Commissioners of the Poor Law in London. It is a plea from distraught people, too proud to beg, being forced to do that very thing in a desperately hopeful letter, probably taken as dictation on their behalf, but heartfelt nonetheless.

> We who sign this letter are the paupers of the parish of Bledlow in Buckinghamshire. We have asked the magistrates at West Wycombe to order the overseers of the poor to give us more relief. They told us that the overseers have no more money to give us and cannot find work for us to enable us to earn better pay.
>
> We are many of us married men with large families. We are all able-bodied men and willing to work, and very unwilling to live in idleness or on charity. There is not one among us who has ever been convicted of any crime, or even accused of any.

And so they set out their stall, proud people, not wanting to beg. The letter continues with an inventory of their pay and requirements for living.

The married men among us are paid 7 shillings a week. In harvest they may earn, for four or perhaps five weeks, as much as 15 shillings a week. The 7 shillings are spent each week as follows:

4s for bread – this will buy a little more than eight quarter loaves.

1s 9d for bacon.

15d for soap, candles, sugar, tea, thread and worsted and such necessaries.

We have nothing left. We have no money remaining for buying clothing or fuel, or to pay for our rent, which is about £3 a year. If we manage to save a guinea out of earning in harvest, it is nearly all spent in paying for our shoes, which cost us 15s or 16s a pair.

Those among us who are single are paid only half a crown a week. This is spent as follows:

13d for 2 quartern loaves.

1s for buying bacon.

2d for lard.

And the rest is sugar, which we mix with water without tea.

We have nothing left to pay for lodging and washing, yet these cost us 10d a week, for which we are obliged to go into debt till chance enables us to pay.

None of us, whether married or single, can buy beer. It is often that we spend weeks without tasting it. Yet we work from seven in the morning till four in the afternoon.

> Several of us have been without food since yesterday evening. When the week is nearly at an end we are very much pinched. On Fridays and Saturdays we scarcely have any bread in the house or money to buy more.

The poor men of Bledlow painted a recognisable picture of what it can be like, living hand-to-mouth on a pittance of a wage, while life piles on, not waiting for you to catch up. However, the ensuing deprivations for them were far greater than even they expected.

> When we married, matters were better. We could, even as children, earn 5s a week. We saved a little out of our wages. We bought furniture and married, not dreaming how the world would turn. Now that we have families about us, we can earn but little more as men than we used to gain as children.
>
> Gentlemen, we have looked for work in vain. We have gone here and there and can find none. Times used to be better for us before Bledlow enclosed. The extensive commons found many of us little comforts.
>
> We, therefore, humbly, entreat you that you will visit our parish without delay, for hunger, cold will not allow delay.
>
> We are, gentlemen, most respectfully and obediently . . .

The appeal was published in *The Times* and Edward Ashworth, a millowner in Bolton, wrote to the Poor Law Commission suggesting that migration to the fast-growing manufacturing districts of the north might help solve this problem. Good, tough, reliable workers were proving hard to find in the mills, and those with ready-made families, eager to work, seemed a perfect solution. Families meant children, and ag lab families meant children who were used to labour, albeit outdoors.

One of the assistant commissioners, a Dr Kay, was sent to Bledlow, where he visited every family, offering employment contracts with certain northern millowners. A general wage of 24 to 30 shillings a week was on offer to an average family containing five or six workers. This compared to their present level of around 7 shillings a week, yet the commissioner complained that his offer 'met with great reluctance' at first. Did the reluctant workers get some inkling of what lay in store for them? Moving your entire family for the kind for work you feel you're cut out for is one thing; to turn your back on your home for something completely out of your experience is another. Yet these were men who saw dignity in honest labour and had passionately petitioned for the opportunity to put bread on their family tables. When we consider that their houses were often nothing more than ruinous cottages, 'little more than a low, dark hut' with mud floors, the hesitation in leaving them seems more baffling. Were they afraid? If so, it seemed that perhaps if a brave few stepped forward and took up the challenge, then the rest would follow. To watch your fellow strugglers pack up their worldly belongings and set off for a new life while you chose to stay behind in abject poverty would have proved a tough and possibly indefensible choice.

In Dr Kay's opinion, many of the migrants were unsuitable because 'their energies and morals alike have been exhausted by a long course of cunning and servile dependence'. He went on to recommend that offers of migration should be made only to those who 'deserved to be extricated from their present situation by the exhibition of superior moral qualities and proof of a superior energy'. Though it's doubtful if hard-pressed parishes would be so picky, sorting industrious wheat from idle, morally reprehensible chaff.

The commissioners decided it was time to take action to control the migrants, and offices were established in Leeds and Manchester. Robert Baker handled the West Riding of Yorkshire from Leeds and, controlling Lancashire, Cheshire and Derbyshire from Manchester, was one Richard Muggeridge. These men set up systems for both the parishes and the millowners and oversaw the whole migration. Over the following eighteen months, they were to oversee the migration of around 660 families, 4,500 people in all. The migration system finished in 1837, three years after the Bledlow letter, just as a five-year depression kicked in across the country.

The first workers to leave had to be the most determined, or the most desperate, piling into the barges and along canals that took them from Bledlow to the unknown north. Their arrival caused great consternation. Even people used to the rigours of poverty were shocked at the state of most of them.

They must have seemed sub-human, staggering ashore, grimy, naked beneath tattered rags and weak from hunger, with the stench of desperation rising from them.

Two of the earliest of Mr Muggeridge's Migrants, as they were known, were men from Bledlow, arriving at Quarry Bank in October 1835: John Stevens, with his wife and nine children, and John Howlett, with his wife and four children. Unlike the orphan apprentices, these children would live in the village with their families. John Howlett signed a contract with the Gregs for him and his children at eleven and a half hours a day for two years, and they all received a wage. Orphaned children in the same group from Bledlow were indentured like all the rest and went straight to the Apprentice House. This must have appeared as an enormous and bitterly unfair gulf in fortunes to the orphans from Bledlow. Still, that's what happened when your parents were dead.

John Howlett is a character with a pivotal role in the second series of the television dramatisation, an early 'working-class Tory' determined that he and his family should earn their way, physically fighting with Daniel Bate as personal convictions battle against political beliefs. In the fiction, he breaks the picket lines in his unwavering belief that a man's right to work should know no bars. In many ways he and Daniel are fighting the same battle, albeit from diametrically opposed stances. Fictionally, Howlett has to be working in the factory to come into such dramatic conflict with Esther and Daniel, and although he did spend two years in the scutching room, where the least able of men and children were put to use, he spent most of his tie in Styal working on the Greg estate, engaged as a cowman-cum-labourer, and so doing very similar work to that he had left behind. So it was the Howlett children who bore the brunt of the shift in occupations, who carried the hopes of a successful migration in their youthful hands. Howlett's three daughters were around the same age as Esther and, along with their little brother, worked in the mill. In their southern homelands, the transition to an adult way of life would have been more gradual. They would have watched their parents work, and appreciated that their time would come and be all the more ready for it. In the mills they were plunged head first into an alien environment. And it was to be too alien for some of the migrants. Despite the awful conditions they'd been living in, some chose to return to the parishes they'd abandoned only months earlier.

It was reported that 'some idle girls of dissolute character' and some young men had returned, citing loneliness as their reason. Whether the girls were dissolute on arrival, or became dissolute while at the mill, is not stated. The Poor Law Commissioners were in no doubt as to the reasons for falling back on the charity of the workhouses: 'some of the individuals, have been inured to parish pay and the reckless loitering life which an habitual dependence on it invariably gives rise to, have failed to acquire regular and industrial habits, and have returned to their former homes'. In other words, they are too lazy to break out of the ruinous cycle of relying on handouts and would prefer to do that rather than do an honest day's labour. This reinforces the Victorians' belief that any signs of weakness, idleness or social misdeeds shown by the working classes were deemed to be their own fault. Of course they would fall into dissolution if left to their own devices – they were, after all, the working classes for a good reason, by circumstance or by way of birth.

Whether children left home by themselves or with their families, one thing is certain: their departure was never anything they had any control over. They had to go where they were told. Whether they made this journey in hope, sorrow, anger or fear, they all arrived in the same place: a melting pot of displaced humanity.

CHAPTER THREE

EARLY DAYS

If the new apprentices had believed the lies, they'd be happy to arrive. They would have welcomed the day when the cart arrived to carry them off to the mill, cheering as they thought of the better life ahead, like a nineteenth-century version of the naughty boys in *Pinocchio*. The foundlings and orphans among them, often as young as six or seven, probably just desired some kind of family life, anything to fill the vacuum of their parents' deaths or desertion. Other new apprentices would be justifiably frightened before they set out, often with simple childish uncertainty and fear. Those with more attitude, like Esther Price, would see the mill as a challenge, something to resist. With her best mate Lucy Garner in tow, she'd come over from Liverpool, that sprawling, bustling port, and its dreadful workhouse. Surely that had prepared her for what Quarry Bank could throw at her?

As the horse-drawn cart took them through the heavily wooded slopes of the valley, they would become aware of a noise, gradually growing in volume. They couldn't see the mill, but they could hear it. It seemed to bellow and belch sound, its heart booming to the hollow drumming of the great wheel as the River Bollin raced through it. The sound promised violence from an unchained beast. 'Listen,' it seemed to growl. 'I devour children.' Any apprentices who were already anxious would be terrified now, their own hearts beating faster. Even those who thought they had reason to be cheerful would cast fearful glances at each other – they knew they were coming to a mill, so how bad could it be?

Whatever thoughts swam through their minds on their way to Quarry Bank Mill, they couldn't have imagined what lay in wait for them within the towering brick walls. Once the factory gates clanged behind them, it would hit them with a sheer visceral shock.

A stay of execution, though, while they were escorted to the Apprentice House, their home for the foreseeable future. Here they would eat, sleep, be schooled, fall ill, fall in love and, possibly, die. It would probably have been the largest house any of them had ever seen, quite grand and imposing. You could hear the mill from here – it was only a five-minute downhill walk away – but it was tantalisingly hidden from view, in its cave of trees. The ivy-clad Apprentice House, set among open fields, boasted its own small kitchen garden, where row upon row of cabbage, potato, carrot and turnip grew. Small outbuildings housing the pigsty and the laundry completed the effect of a working farm, rather than a home to over eighty children and their custodians.

The old building has been lovingly and authentically

restored. Exploring it today, you can experience all the sights, sounds and smells that must have washed over every new apprentice. The heavy click of a latch lets you into the schoolroom, with its simple wooden benches and tables, and you breathe in the tang of woodsmoke that lingers in the air. Hanging on the walls are tapestries of the Lord's Prayer and simple alphabets, all but indecipherable to most new arrivals. They'd stay like that for the girls, who were taught to sew but not to read (though a few did manage to acquire some skill, as we shall see). The boys were taught to read, and perform simple mathematical tasks. They would start to learn using their fingers to draw in sand. Only the older, more proficient, were eventually allowed the luxury of a quill and ink, and a scrap of precious paper once they'd practised on slates.

From this room, narrow staircases lead to the dorms, one large room for sixty girls and three smaller rooms for the boys. They slept apart, separated by the snapping to of the latch, the slip of a bolt, a simple turn of the key. The house is an echo chamber for noise. At night, preparing for bed, sitting on your makeshift mattress of coarse cloth and straw that shifts itchily beneath your weight, you can hear every sound. The clatter of clogs on the wooden floors, the shuffling, whispering and shifting of bodies. The fall and rise of wheezing, whistling chests . . . Were it not for your sheer exhaustion, sleep might have proved elusive.

The girls' room has two huge arched windows at either end, tall enough to allow a fully grown man to stand in them. One window overlooks the garden, the other looks towards

Styal. Even though in Esther's day the windows were smaller, they would still have been the apprentices' eyes on their world, though shaking in a strong wind and offering scant protection from the cold. You can stand close to them and feel the wind's icy breath on your face. In humid, sticky summers the windows would blaze with sunlight and the house would funnel the accumulated heat into the roof areas, turning the dorms into saunas of pooling sweat.

Both sexes slept two to a bed. Sharing a bed would be no novelty for children used to huddling up with other paupers or random siblings. It was not the practice to allow friends to sleep together. You had no choice in the matter. Tough, if you were stuck with a crybaby or a bed-wetter, worse still if you were one yourself.

There are communal pisspots, each next to a bale of straw, which would have been used for both extra bedding and, presumably, to give some protection for those wiping their backsides. Right-handed children would soon learn to use their left hands as their 'cack hands', reserving the right one, the 'puddin' hand', for the thick dollop of porridge slapped into it every morning. Not a good idea to get them mixed up. This earthy image of the porridge landing with a slap into the open palms of the children was one of the first we saw in the very first episode of the television series. Although there is no documented evidence of this practice, who would have had time to wash up to a hundred porridge bowls each day? Would the overlookers simply have tapped their fingers patiently as the workers spooned every last morsel into their mouths? Highly unlikely. Your hands were what you ate with, pure and simple. Left-handers were soon forced from their natural bent. There are records of children having their left hands tied behind them to promote use of their right hands, left-handedness being seen as unnatural or as a sign of some sort of mental deficiency. Harsh treatment but not uncommon and quite widespread, still being inflicted into the 1920s.

Simple wooden pegs hammered into the walls over the cots were used for any discarded clothing. Children had one set of simple work clothes, coarse cotton jackets and trousers, or pinafores, and wooden clogs. The work clothes were worn all week, and changed only in time for the wearing of the Sunday best for visits to the church of St Bart's in Wilmslow. Personal hygiene was not a lifestyle choice. Only the parts of their skin already exposed to the elements had a quick splash from the freezing water in the well. You wouldn't know it now, walking through the rooms, but the whole Apprentice House must have been suffused with the funk of rancid human sweat and the tang of the mechanical oily residue that soaked into work clothes. There's a clue in the form of the many sprigs of dried herbs and flowers hanging from rafters and beams throughout the house. Back in the days of our apprentices, though, these floral air fresheners would have had only a token effect on the cloying atmosphere.

A large kitchen sits at the rear of the house, adjoining the back yard where the water pump sits. This must have been the apprentices' favourite room, with its comforting warmth, porridge bubbling on the hob – and, on occasion, the riotously delicious aroma of bacon. But this was not a place for children to enjoy. The kitchen's purpose was to provide fuel to keep the apprentices going, to see them through their arduous days, one dollop of gruel at a time.

All new apprentices had to go before the mill's doctor, the renowned Dr Peter Holland from Knutsford. Most of these children would never have even seen a doctor, let alone be examined by one. And they could have no idea just how unusual it was that he should be there in the first place. It was unheard-of for any millowner to provide medical treatment for his workers, yet Samuel Greg paid Holland a retainer of £20 per year. The children also couldn't know just how distinguished Holland was. Not only a celebrated and respected doctor, moving in the same social circles as the Gregs (and the uncle of the celebrated novelist Mrs Gaskell), he was also the first to make meticulous records of his treatments and patients. These handwritten notes exist as part of the archive, and are considered by no less a body than the World Health Organisation to be the first records of industrial health. Even though Samuel and Hannah Greg, along with Holland himself, didn't know it, they were making history.

Dr Holland's initial examination of the new apprentices was thorough. Eyelids would be peeled back, mouths cranked open, ears probed, teeth tested. Joints flexed, lungs listened to, nothing perfunctory, everything noted. From his records, we see that of the 292 children first examined, the breakdown of his diagnoses was as follows:

203 Healthy
32 Delicate
28 Inflammation of the eyes
7 Enlarged glands
4 Scrofulous
4 Under age
3 Old injuries (arms, fingers, legs)
1 Scurvy
1 Bed wetter
1 Weak intellect
1 Dwarfish
1 Discharging
1 Weak ankle
1 Unhealthy
4 Feverish

The term 'scrofulous' infers a swelling of the lymph glands and, in the time of Dr Holland, would have been thought to be tuberculosis.

So, those 203 healthy apprentices passed the test and were in. What about the others? While the Gregs were exceptionally considerate employers, compared to their peers, the mill was a business, not a hospital. Many children would have watched as some poor souls were discarded like undersized fish and returned, at the expense of the parish, to the workhouse they came from. Such as Clara Harrison, aged ten, from Liverpool: 'Has enlarged glands. Had better not be engaged at present.' For such sickly children, there would have been a terribly ironic fear of rejection – please let me be passed fit. Fit for a life of unremitting toil.

It was different for a child whose ailment promised to clear up. There are documented cases where apprentices have been kept on until they have recovered from whatever affected them on arrival, as this note attests: 'Sarah Powell, Liverpool. Aged 9. Healthy now. Had inflamed eyes a year ago but they are well now and there does not seem to be any objection to engaging her.' Mystifyingly, Esther Price's name appears in the mill doctor's notebook as early as 3 May 1831, two and a half years before her indenture. Was she tossed back into the horrors of the workhouse? If she was it would make sense of her determination never to go back there, unless, typically Esther, it was under her own terms. Dr Holland's notes first describe her as 'delicate', yet by 16 May 1831, he writes that Esther did 'appear better'. Why then wait another two years before signing her indenture? Clearly Samuel Greg felt she was worth the wait. Though probably not the way she was to repay him: violent conduct in 1835, running away in 1836, being locked up with the dead Mrs Timperley, drawing the attention of the Short Time Committee and successfully proving that her age had been wrongly registered. Hardly the acts of a 'delicate' young woman.

So, some calculated risks were taken, but not the kind that might not pay off. Unwell children whose siblings were at work in the mill, though, would be given extra time to recover. Was this born out of a desire to care for the wellbeing of the child or simply an expedient means of keeping those working happy, or at least not unhappy, less anxious about their brothers and sisters and more able to concentrate on working? Probably somewhere in between. The Gregs may well have not wanted to split families up for humanitarian reasons; but of course a family more used to the environment would more readily stay around, lending a kind of longevity to the life span of the workforce.

A look at Dr Holland's writings from 1789 gives us an idea of what happened to those new arrivals.

> August 1st
> *John Mop* Let him go on with the wash to the neck and continue to bath in the river.
>
> August 16th
> *Hannah Riley* Let her bath every day in the River. Let a bread and milk poultice be applied to the leg each morning and night. Let a wet cloth with cold spring water be applied to the neck. Keeping the cloth constantly wet. Let her take two sowerdrops three times a day in a little water.
>
> *Martha Davenport* Let the inside of each shoe be raised nearly half an inch.
>
> August 24th
> *Hannah Riley* Let her go on with the sowerdrops and continue with the poultice to the leg and wet cloth to the neck. Let her take 15 of the drops for a dose gradually increasing to 20 drops.

September 6th

Edward Thursfield Let more leeches be applied just below the eye. Let a blister be applied to the back of the neck and remaining on for 24 hours. Let him continue to apply the cold water to the eye and take the powder and salts as before directed.

Hannah Riley Let two tablespoons of vinegar be added to make one pint of water. The poultice to be made with this instead of milk and applied cold to the leg. Let her go on with the sowerdrops.

William Sargent Let him take one dose of the white powders at night and in the morning a dose of senna. Let him repeat this every other day.

Arabella Watkins Let her take two grammes of St James' powder every six hours and keep in bed at present drinking plentiful of thin drinks, common tea, whey etc.

Some of these medicines, if we can call them that, need explanation. Sowerdrops translate as just that, sour drops, like acid drops, supposed to aid indigestion. When Dr Holland tells us that 'a blister' should be applied, again his meaning is literal. An object such as a stone, or sometimes a sixpence, would be heated over the range and then placed directly on the patient, in this case poor Edward Thursfield, until it produced a blister. When the blister had fully formed and was full of pus, it was cut off. This was a common practice, based on the belief that the gathered pus actually contained whatever infection was making the patient ill. For example, on the neck for sore throats, on the forehead for headaches, and under the armpit, near the glands, for a general infection.

When you take a tour of the present-day Apprentice House you are treated to a close examination of some of Dr Holland's standard medicines, including the leeches. Of course these days, the leeches are 'organically' sourced, bringing to mind marsh after marsh of leech farms, and, once they've had their fifteen minutes of fame, are returned safely from whence they came. A perusal of the A–Z of Dr Holland's medical arsenal leaves you in no doubt that some of the children did well to survive the cure, let alone the initial illness. Here's a selection:

Anondyne antimonial pills: antimony is similar to arsenic and is just as poisonous. This was used to induce vomiting.

Barley water: a cure for cystitis.

Bladder: exactly that. A sheep or pig's bladder, used as a hot water bottle. If there wasn't a bladder to hand, hot bricks were used.

Colocynth blus pills: a 'drastic cathartic'.

Goose grease: used for smearing on sore chests.

Jalap: another purgative with side effects of 'griping'.

James' powders, or St James's powders: used as an emetic, to induce vomiting and sweating.

Nitrate of silver: a caustic agent, used to burn off warts and verrucas.

Opium (and laudanum): need no introduction, and even poppy heads turn up on the list, said to be 'hypnotic'. A heady combination of drugs, presumably only used in cases of extreme pain and discomfort.

Quicklime: another caustic agent, along with sulphur ointment.

Sixpenny piece: often used as a way of measuring the powders. An amount was piled on to a sixpence, and no more, and this was deemed to be the correct measure.

Water from the smithy: taken after hot irons had been cooled many times in it, it was said then to be rich in iron itself and was used for anaemia.

White ointment: a mixture of white beeswax and white paraffin.

On the whole most cures seemed to involve bleeding, letting and purging. If something infected or bad was clearly inside you, it had to come out, from one orifice or another – and, as far as work was concerned, the sooner the better. The records also show that whatever their condition, all the new children were given 'two pills and a white powder' on their first day. What were they for? Quarry Bank volunteer and local chemist Philip Charnley has a ready and plausible explanation. They would have been used for worming the children. Philip can trace his own ancestors back 200 years in Styal, and remembers many of the potions and remedies used on the child apprentices still being requested over the counter of his father's chemist shop in the 1950s. Other extracts note that often the child's hair was cut short, presumably as a remedy for lice. This of course would have been dreaded by the girls who, with precious few possessions of their own, prided themselves on their hair.

Having made the initial examination, Holland would leave most of the day-to-day work to junior doctors, and certainly left the reading, interpretation and administering of his recommendations to the stewards of the Apprentice House. The fact that most of these people couldn't read meant that Hannah Greg took it upon herself to visit and read out the prescriptions. Later, when they were old enough, she took her daughters with her, encouraging them to look upon the apprentices as people deserving of their attentions and help. Again, absolutely unheard-of compared to the cotton mills of Manchester and Nottingham.

The new apprentices had another ordeal, but a vital one: inoculation against smallpox. An outbreak of any debilitating disease in the Apprentice House would have proved disastrous and, of all the possible candidates, smallpox was feared the most. Dr Edward Jenner had been one of the first to realise that infection from the mild disease of cowpox (caught, naturally enough, from cows) conferred immunity from the deadly smallpox. He developed his method of 'vaccination' (from the Latin for 'cow') during the late 1790s, against much initial scepticism and outright hostility. 'A cure for our most virulent disease, from the pus of a farm animal?' What's more, according to the clergy it was positively 'ungodly' to take material from a diseased animal. Fortunately, Jenner persevered, and by 1804 a vaccine was in common use. By 1826, it was being regularly administered at Quarry Bank.

So, having survived the medical examination and been inoculated, what now for the new apprentices? The mill was waiting.

There it stood: a massive bulk, 160 feet long, 30 feet wide and five storeys high, and pulsating with that unmistakable noise. If the children's arrival coincided with a rare break from work, they would have seen the shuffling forms of the present workers filing past. Veterans of thirteen or fourteen, with waxen and pallid complexions, knees buckled, hands scarred, fingers bent or missing. These wretches would gaze back at the newcomers, some of them fresh from the farm and rosy-cheeked, though forsaken by parents racked with debt. Knowing glances would be exchanged and implicit warnings given. Don't look on us with pity, for soon we will all look the same. And, up close to these seemingly alien creatures, another sensory introduction to life at the mill: the smell. This came off the workers in waves, a rancid cocktail of sweat, oil and grease. The smell of the beast.

Inside the huge building, the beast took form. Great shadowy machines flexed their muscles through a fog of flax and haze of dust. Their deafening clatter could not be shouted over and apprentices signalled with their hands, a semaphore of the downtrodden. With the day starting at 5.30am and ending at 8pm, the vast machinery rooms would be lit by what light spilled through the waxen windows. The ante-rooms, lit by tallow candle, did little to alleviate the gloom but much to add to the stench with their sickly, oily perfume. Here in this half-lit world, and to the cacophonous orchestra of the machines, the smallest children whipped in and out of the bellies of the rhythmically chiming looms like so many deranged spiders, forever weaving the same intricate webs, then fleeing with seconds to spare. To the newcomers the work seemed appallingly dangerous and impossibly quick, but also unendurably hard and seemingly unending.

How could anyone spend more than a few seconds in the same space as so much brutal machinery making so much ear-splitting noise? Then the newcomers would notice that those already at work sported hand-made ear plugs, fashioned from the cotton fibres that swirled around them like a snowstorm. The heat hit them next, often scaling the 70–90 degrees Fahrenheit mark, causing rivulets of sweat to course down their faces, tear-like, through the swiftly caking effect of the dust and cotton. The children scampered about, wearing their simple work clothes but barefoot. Apprentices learned quickly to shed their protective wooden clogs. The threat of a spark from the metal nails in this tinderbox environment was unthinkable. Besides, the last thing you needed when scampering away from the looming machinery was to slip and be caught and mangled. No, bare feet were so much safer. The newcomers must have marvelled at their efforts while being aghast – how was this work done, sixteen hours a day, day in, day out?

We have useful clues from the words of apprentices themselves. Among the records of life at both the Apprentice House and the mill are testimonies from runaways, who, when they were caught, had to answer to the local Justice of the Peace. Running away was such a grave crime in the eyes of authority that it gets a whole chapter to itself later in this book. For now, the recorded testimony of Joseph Sefton, who ran away to London with fellow apprentice Thomas Priestly in 1806, gives some idea of daily life at Quarry Bank.

He had arrived at the mill in a group of eight boys and four girls from the London parish of Hackney and claims to have been thirteen and a half at the date of his indenture. He tells the court in Chester that there were 42 boys in the house at that time and more girls. He relates that 'the rooms were very clean the floors washed frequently'. Also that the rooms were 'aired daily and whitewashed once a year'. So much for the remedies, but not enough to regularly tackle the cause. Joseph also gives us a taste of the simple fare offered from the kitchen:

> On Sunday we had for dinner boiled pork and potatoes. We also had peas, beans, turnips and cabbages in their season
>
> Monday — We had dinner milk and bread and sometimes thick porridge. We always had as much as we could eat
>
> Tuesday — We had milk and potatoes
>
> Wednesday — Sometimes bacon and potatoes and sometimes milk and bread

Thursday	If we had bacon on Wednesday then we had bread and milk
Friday	We used to have lob scouse
Saturday	We used to dine on thick porridge

We had only water to drink, when ill we were allowed tea

Lob scouse was a very common dish in the area, a vegetable stew sometimes with added pork, especially popular in Liverpool (presumably influenced by the many sailors in and out of the port) –hence the term 'Scousers'.

This testimony speaks of reasonable nourishment and conditions for the time, but, as with other documents attesting to the good treatment at Quarry Bank, we must take into account the circumstances under which they were given. Most descriptions were given by captured runaways, keen to atone for their misconduct and mindful of the fines awaiting them, paid for by many extra hours of overtime at a penny an hour.

Joseph goes on describe his work: 'I was first employed to drop bobbins (that is, taking a full bobbin off the spindle and putting an empty one on). I then saved straps and put these round the binders (the straps twisted the lists and the lists turned the wheels). I used to oil the machinery every morning.' This simple account does not stray into the conditions under which the work was carried out, and this is a recurring theme, an economy with the truth that lends credence to the later analysis by Frederick Engels in his *The History of the Working Class in England*. He wrote this seminal book after observing appalling conditions in Manchester, the hub of the Industrial Revolution, in the early 1840s. He maintained that workers could become under some spell of 'beguiling slavery'. The closest Joseph comes to complaining is when he states, 'I like my employment very well I was obliged to make overtime every night but I did not like this as I wanted to learn my book . . . I wanted to go oftener to school than twice a week including Sundays but Richard Bamford would not let me go tho' the mill had stopped but this was the time that the straps and frames wanted mending.'

So he sugars the pill of not wanting to be enslaved to the machines that needed tending even when idle by claiming it only impeded his thirst for knowledge. Noble aspirations or simply seeking respite from the hell of the work floor by any means, even school? He notably keeps the Greg name out of the equation, naming Bamford, the overlooker, instead. Still, brave words, as the overlookers were regarded as people to be feared and respected in equal measure – they held your fate in their hands on a daily basis, whereas the Gregs were looked on as gods. Gentlefolk who occasionally alighted from heaven to chastise, educate and put them to work. The Gregs provided their whole world: food, clothes, punishment, education, housing, medicine, money. They were literally lords of everything they surveyed and many apprentices knew nothing beyond what the Gregs allowed them to.

The account of another child apprentice, Job Baker, should also be viewed as the truth, but not the whole truth. His recollections were documented by HM Medical Inspector of

Factories, one R. Murray, in response to *The History of Robert Blincoe* which, as we have seen, exposed the conditions endured in the workhouse by young Robert. The book also describes his later years working in the nearby mill at Litton, where horrendous practices were commonplace, as we shall see. Job's memoirs are supposed to redress the balance, and certainly his start at the mill is unusually – maybe uniquely – upbeat.

Job's history before joining the mill, in May 1822, has a familiar ring. His older sister Mary had already been at the mill for six years, starting soon after their father died at Waterloo, leaving the family destitute in their home town of Burslem. Then their mother had died, shortly after giving birth to their brother George, who remained with Job in the workhouse at nearby Congleton. When it was Job's turn to leave, George remained behind (later to blaze a trail of his own and end up in deep trouble).

Job's first day offered no hint of what was waiting for him within the mill's booming walls. A rather pleasant ride in a cart took him through the countryside between Congleton and Styal, past the rustic villages of Marton and Siddington and through the heart of Alderley Edge and the rural idyll of Redesmere. In May, this journey would have been a glorious reminder of how beautiful the Cheshire countryside could be. Fields blazing with golden rape, shady woodlands of oak and ash carpeted with spring bluebells and meadows lush with poppy. Arriving first at the Apprentice House, he was given a bowl of porridge with treacle in it. Then he received his two sets of clothes. His working suit of an old jacket and trousers had been mended carefully, having been passed down from an older, bigger apprentice. Job considered his Sunday suit 'very grand', made as it was from 'dark green fustian with red collars and a high-crowned hat'. Both suits were to last Job two years, if indeed he himself lasted that long.

Apparently Dr Holland took a shine to Job, 'patted him on the head', telling him he was a 'healthy young specimen' who need not fear not being taken on. Job was then allowed to stroll around on his own, and set off towards the sound of the mill. This was to be the last time he ever walked this path with such a light heart. He noticed the muted roar of the Bollin in full spate and saw the magnificent Greg mansion, its back to the road and surrounded by tiered mature gardens of rhododendrons, cedars, fruit trees and exotic conifers. He even noticed deer wandering through the grounds, and watched the Bollin snake through the land and away towards Wilmslow, disappearing into towering woods.

All apprentices making their way to and from the mill, often in the dark, would pass close to the rear windows of the Greg house on this route. As you stroll through the interior of the house you notice that the bedrooms facing the garden and river are the grandest, including that of Samuel and Hannah. Those at the rear are the smallest and, as such, must have housed their many children. In winter, with the bushes sparse, it is possible to see the road to the mill clearly. In this way it's also possible to see the bedroom windows. How many times must the desperate and exhausted apprentice children looked longingly at these windows and how many times must the clatter of their clogs have brought an inquisitive Greg child to them, anxious for a glimpse at what must have seemed beings from another world, hard to believe they were human? In summer the rhododendrons bloomed into barriers, a riot of blue and purple, blotting out the house and putting a seasonal end to the furtive glimpses.

Murray's *Reply to Robert Blincoe* says that Job's first day was enhanced further by the appearance of old Sam Henshall, whose son was the mill's engineer. The Henshalls have a rich history at Quarry Bank, some descendants still volunteering at the mill to this day. Sam took it upon himself to give the new lad a tour of the mechanics, the heart of the beast, and the first ever door Job went through delivered him to the very bowels of the great building.

Again, all apprentices would have heard the wheel before they got anywhere near it, that impossibly deep boom. A small wooden door off a mossy cobbled alleyway gives way to an enormous, almost subterranean cavern, many degrees cooler and dripping with river water. The immense iron wheel takes the breath away: 32 feet in diameter, 21 feet wide and weighing 44 tons, it seems impossible that anything could move it, let alone the mere flow of a river. But here it was, turning to the thrust of water from a tunnel, blasted through solid rock and funnelling the Bollin from where it had been diverted, over half a mile away. By 1822 the wheel didn't shoulder all the tremendous effort it required to power the mill, and Sam Henshall showed Job the steam engine at the other end of the building. Here it was as hot as the cavern had been cool, and water dripped again, but this time as steam, cooling on the ceiling. The engine hissed and spat and pummelled itself at a terrific rate, powering the enormous rocking beam – as modern and muscular as the wheel seemed ancient and immovable.

As evening encroached, Job stepped back up the lane, his head spinning with the wonder of what he had seen, halting only to be questioned by 'a grand lady and gentleman' who asked him who he was and where he'd come from. Job was described as being 'covered with confusion but he managed to stammer out a few answers then he fled as fast as his legs would carry him'. Chances are these fine gentlefolk were the Gregs, possibly Samuel and Hannah themselves.

Could Job ever have imagined how this day would be the last he enjoyed this kind of freedom and wonder? If not, then he was soon to sample the reality of what his time in the mill would be like, and this day would take on the quality of a dream. The first pin to prick this bubble of illusion was surely the sight of the apprentices, dragging their lead-heavy limbs up that same road, coughing and wheezing all the while. He must have looked out for his sister Mary, but with no luck. Maybe she was avoiding him, putting off that awful moment when he would doubtless ask her what the mill was like. How could she have embraced and welcomed him, knowing all too well what dangers lay in his path?

Job did manage to see Mary fleetingly after supper of 'boiled pork, potatoes and beans' (but did not tell of their conversation), before being ushered up to the male side of the upper floors of the house. Allotted his bunk of rough cloth and straw, he would lay there for the first time with a complete stranger, listening to the turning of the key locking them in. The stink on his sleeping partner, that musky stew of oil and grease, would have contrasted sharply with the reek from the pisspots. Those dried switches of herbs and flowers from the garden, nailed to the beams, would have done little to alleviate the fug settling over the bedrooms. The next day would bring the toil and would help explain the deadened look in Mary's eyes, glimpsed in that all too brief meeting the night before, and the shock of seeing the others at the outside well, snowy with cotton from head to toe, flushing it from their faces with icy water. He'd heard the bellowing of the beast, witnessed its iron lungs and its hissing, metallic, pumping heart. At dawn the next day every apprentice, new or old, would enter its lair. It would have been another wonder the youngest and least experienced children had slept at all.

Five o'clock brought the dreaded ringing of the factory bell, summoning them from their hard cots. A hasty splash from the freezing well water followed by the clammy slap of porridge into their icy hands. After his first night among strangers Job would have been searching the pale, hollow-eyed faces that bobbed around the yard in the early morning gloom like so many moon-shaped lanterns, seeking Mary's friendly features. Then the scatter down the hill, more than a hundred clogs sounding a tattoo over the cobbles as the bell rang insistently. Too late and Mr Greg would shut the gates on you and you'd be fined for the privilege.

Five-thirty saw them shuffle into the mill, ears ringing with the noise, eyes blinking at the snowstorm that swirled around them. Described as 'dazed', Job was allowed to stay with Mary, following her as she worked. He was lucky. Those first days were the most dangerous – an unfolded cuff, a loose shirt sleeve, tails that trailed from the pants; anything that the relentless machines could snatch, they would, ripping and clawing at you, trying to bleed you until you died.

Mary showed him how to 'piece up', the apparently simple job of joining broken threads of yarn as they whipped off the bobbins. This was the most common of the apprentice jobs, especially for newcomers. But when faced with hundreds of bobbins, humidity so fierce that the air stopped in your throat, the streaming of your eyes, the battering noise . . .

Job made it to breakfast at eight-thirty, when he was 'very glad' the work had stopped and they were let out for a bowl of bread and milk, eaten on a grassy bank overlooking the mill. Once outside, it must have been difficult to stir their limbs and get back to their feet to face the mill rooms again. The bewildering cacophony of noise was very real, as was the threat of violence emanating from the swirling, clattering machines. Real fear constricts the throat and stirs the bowels, telling you not to go back in. But, of course, this was not an option and they were all back on the floor until twelve-thirty, by now completing seven hours of back-breaking toil. Lunch was taken after a haul up the hill, past the Greg mansion and back into the Apprentice House. A hastily gobbled meal of bacon, potatoes and greens before rushing back to the relentless grind for one-thirty. More bread and milk at five where they worked, then on and on.

The apprentices must have yearned for a sight of the outside world, trying to snatch a glimpse out of the mill windows, especially on the river side. Maybe on a trip to the privy, one per room, and fashioned from simple, worn wood; ironically, it offered little privacy. A quick stop to rub an already filthy cuff against the greasy, fluff-grimed pane would allow a view over the tumbling Bollin beneath, across the adjacent meadow. To the south you can see the raging weir as the river begins to be harvested for its power, a muddy, foamy beard of water, creating a pool of whirling spume. To the north you can just make out the very edges of the Greg mansion, Quarry Bank House, the terraces spilling down to the river, which, as it weaves through this land, seems almost respectful in its pace, tamed as it were by the presence of gentry. The more likely answer being that the mill has drained the Bollin of any real power and allows it to slide through the Greg gardens in an ornamental fashion. On certain days the opportunistic apprentice might also catch a glimpse of the Greg family, mainly the women, as they strolled through these gardens and terraces, completely unaware of the turmoil taking place behind each oily pane of the mill. They may have seen the Greg children playing, running carefree amongst the mature rhododendrons and hiding in the hermit's cave, a mouth of reddish sandstone yawning above the gardens. These would have been stolen seconds before turning unwillingly away or, more likely, being hauled back to the floor by an angry overlooker and thrust back into the cauldron of the workfloor.

On the Styal side of the mill any secret observer would have seen the yardsmen at work, loading carts with finished goods, to be transported to far-off places, places tantalisingly beyond the reach of the apprentices. Once in a while, though, they might get a taste of this outside world themselves. In his *Reply to Robert Blincoe*, Murray describes other days in the life of Job Baker and his workmates. When the Bollin was low, apprentices could either escape the watchful eye of Matthew Fawkner, the mill manager, or be put to further use. The young lads met with 'pack-horse men carrying salt from Northwich' and heard tales of the 'campaigns of the great Duke of Wellington'. On other occasions they would travel with the carter, 'taking yarn to the hand-loom weavers in Lacey Green and Wilmslow'. These would have been great escapades compared to the drudgery of mill life. The lads would have returned to the Apprentice House, leaving their peers agape with the retelling of these stories, whispered in the darkness of the dorm and, no doubt, occasionally embellished by the teller.

Back to Job's first day. The torture didn't end till eight o'clock, although some would stay for overtime at a penny an hour, trying to pay off fines or even build up a store of their own money. Job didn't stay. Instead, according to the account, he leaned heavily on Mary, close to dropping with fatigue as they staggered up the hill and back to the Apprentice House. There Job would see for the first time how he'd become a snowman just like all the others, as he bent over the well and saw his reflection. He'd quickly swill his face, but no amount of water would wash away the cotton fibres already beginning to line his throat. Tiny spidery threads, reaching and connecting, building a nest around his lungs.

It wouldn't seem possible that even more was demanded of them, but now it was time for schooling, learning to sew or to read and do sums. That night Job would have fallen gratefully into his cot, the stink already beginning to feel less alien, everything seeming to matter less. The spark would already have begun to fade from his youthful eyes, his pallor quickening, breath coming shorter.

Welcome to the mill, his body was telling him. Welcome to your new life.

CHAPTER FOUR

Nuts and Bolts

Those displaced humans were to be found at every level of the mill, in every process, especially after the weaving sheds were built on site, in 1835. From then on Quarry Bank Mill encompassed the whole process of production, from taking in the raw cotton to shipping out the finished cloth. Any newcomer, like Job Baker, would have marvelled at just how many people toiled over the machinery and scurried between the mill's buildings, like so many ants swarming over a hill. If he was in any doubt as to his place in this unspoken hierarchy, Job only had to glance at the huge gears turning the wheels' momentum into raw power. Of all the cogs making up these elaborate mechanisms, apprentices like Job were the smallest, least significant – worker ants. Yet without even the smallest cog, a machine is useless. In many ways new apprentices were similar to the raw cotton being baled into the warehouse. They needed to be torn asunder, reconstructed and moulded to the mill's needs. In the way that the cotton had to be prepared for spinning, so the apprentices had to be readied for their tasks, as they could be thrust into any of the cotton's progress as it wound its way through the mill.

Spinning is an arduous process, with the cotton undergoing many refinements before being deemed ready for weaving. Raw cotton was sent out from the southern states of America, densely packed into weighty bales, around five feet tall and a yard across. Once unloaded at Liverpool docks, they were taken by cart to the mill, where they were stacked on the ground floor as they were too heavy to be lifted any higher. They first had to be unpacked in the warehouse, the tightly compressed cotton torn out by hand. I stand alongside my guide, Chris Guffogg, the Premises and Engineering Manager at Quarry Bank, awed by the solidity of the cotton bale before me. Chris peels back a corner of the rough hemp covering, exposing the snowy white cotton underneath. He invites me to pluck some out and I begin to probe with my fingers, expecting little resistance. The raw cotton is soft to the touch but, when I tried plunging my own fingers into it, I find it almost impossible, so densely was it packed. Fingernails must have been bent back and broken to the quick. Each large bale had to be loosened as quickly as possible by the children. They must have plucked at it like demented woodpeckers, as if their very lives depended on it; pinching the wispy surface and feeling it snap frustratingly with the effort as they tried to lengthen the strand they'd just spent precious minutes trying to extricate.

Next stop was the huge scutching room, one of the most feared places of work in the entire industry. Here, machines would pulverise the cotton into shreds of submission, cleansing it of seeds and dust and other impurities. Each machine stands taller than a man and is around twenty feet in length. When they heave into action, the floor trembles beneath your feet as the cotton is fed remorselessly into the mouth of the roaring scutching machine. Inside, drums lined with nails and razor-like teeth tear at the cotton as it passes through. The air quickly fills with a fog so deep it becomes impossible to see to the end of the room. Your ears ring with the sound of metal ripping and grinding. The wheels and belts driving the machine whirl away rapidly, inches from your body. Standing today, as close as you are allowed to, and even encased in Health and Safety cladding, they beckon. Gunmetal grey and glistening with oil, deadly. Imagine then, a room with ten of these beasts standing side by side, forcing you to turn your body sideways as you tried to squeeze between them, all whirling and screaming in unison, reaching out for anything to grab, any chance to whip you into their lethal embrace. If they seem to lunge at your front, you wouldn't dare bend away, for fear of what lay in wait, inches from your back.

The heat generated here meant that most workers stripped to their underwear, though comfort wasn't the only consideration. Close-fitting clothes meant that the machines had less to snatch at, unless it was your very skin. In these devilish rooms, the work was so dangerous that only the lowliest of workers were placed there, those deemed 'not the full shilling'. And, of course, the children. It would have been bad enough to find yourself in a place of great danger, worse still to find yourself at the mercy of someone, who was, in all probability, less skilled or resourceful than yourself.

On the top of the scutching machine you can see two inlet pipes, a little bigger than your thumb. I have their use explained to me by Chris Guffogg. They were introduced at the beginning of the nineteenth century, and would have had hosepipes screwed into them with a ready flow of water waiting to be turned on. Any sign of fire and the operator would hit a foot pedal, instantly flooding the machine with life-saving water.

'What used to happen before?' I ask Chris.

His reply is succinct. 'You ran for your life.'

The air would become so thick with cotton fibres that they could instantly combust and fill the huge room with an explosion of fire. To be honest, running would have been almost futile for some. With one door in and one door out, anyone in the middle wouldn't have got within yards of the doors before they felt the blistering breath of the flames searing at their unclothed backs. This is why every worker and owner feared a fire. The whole mill would have been up in flames within minutes, lives lost, fortunes gone. This is why the scavenging in and under machines was essential. Cleanliness was not only next to godliness, it was what prevented you meeting your maker well before your time. It's a testament to the apprentices' crippling, assiduous work rate that there was never a fire of any magnitude at Quarry Bank.

Their aggressive work done, the scutching machines would then spit out the pummelled cotton in a compressed roll known as a lap. These laps were then transferred to the carding rooms, where any remaining impurities would be torn out. The carding process was marginally less dangerous than scutching, but created no less foul an atmosphere. The carding machines seem to squat on the floor like malignant toads, huge drums at their middle. Their noise and fury boomed around the rooms, with a smog so thick it turned you into a snowman, clinging to your eyes, clogging your singing ears and thickening in your lungs. The carding process also separated the cotton into fibres, filed in parallel lines, readied for the spinning. These were spooled into cans, as big as a small child. Once full, these cans had to be hurried onto the next process, always by the children. A single can, not delivered on time, meant a gap in the synchronicity of the process (a literal illustration of the phrase, 'carrying the can'). Any child under the age of twelve or so would struggle to wrap their skinny arms around the can's circumference, waddling as fast as they could between the machines.

Today you can watch as schoolchildren, as carefree as a day off school can make them and dressed entertainingly as mill urchins, scurry the length of the carding room, clutching an empty can, sometimes bigger than themselves, and surefooted in Nike or Adidas. They smile at the effort, laughing at their friends as they wait their turn. No bellowing overlooker waiting for them at the other end, just a smiling, encouraging teacher standing by the side of one of the many safety rails now erected. Of course there's no way you could possibly place a modern child in the real atmosphere of a nineteenth-century mill – it wouldn't even start to be legal. Still, the working mill does its best to educate these visiting children. Any time given in reflection, pausing to think and trying to imagine yourself in the place of the apprentices, is time well spent. Those who fully appreciate what it must have been like in those days will have taken away a lesson they would not soon forget.

Suddenly Chris Guffogg puts his hands up to his face, palms open, as if splashing water over himself. He's showing me how millworkers would mutely ask their mates, what time is it? Woe betide anyone mistakenly covering their mouths, though. This was a sure sign that they were talking about someone, probably you. Not that anyone could actually hear a single word spoken above the factory noise, but those surviving long enough on the factory floors would soon learn to lip read, no matter what their regional accent. Perversely, if you were going to slag someone off, you were probably safer saying it out loud back at the Apprentice House, and in an accent so foreign to the ears of a Scouser like Esther that she would struggle to get the full meaning. Although clearly, as signified by the kind of scrapes she got herself into, somewhere along the line she understood only too well what people were saying about her. Say anything on the mill floor and your fellow workers would read it instantly. Chris tells me one of his father's memories. 'He'd be coming home on the bus, on the top deck, and he'd see people waiting at the stops beneath him. He could understand every word they said.'

I wondered how the mill was lit before the introduction of

gas lighting, and especially in the rooms packed with machinery and workers. When I ask Chris, he says, 'They weren't.' The tallow candles, moulded from pig fat, were not allowed anywhere near the mill rooms. Only the murky light spilling in from the small windows would have seeped into the working areas. You simply worked dawn to dusk. The whole effect must have been like working underwater, in the filthiest of ponds, with small pools of light that faded and died away just a few feet from entering through the grimy windows. Eyes stinging, ears assailed by the howling machinery, head thumping and your bare, splintered feet desperately seeking purchase as you dodged down aisles of snapping metal. Hour after hour, day after day, year after year. As a visitor, you leave the carding and scutching rooms a chastened person, the mill floor vibrating beneath your feet.

Just when I think that the cotton must now surely be ready for weaving, Chris swiftly disabuses me. He reels off process after process, each designed to stretch and refine the cotton fibres. Evocative words cascade through his explanation: pirns, rovings, creels, beamers, until I am dizzy with the complexity of it all. Yet at heart it is a simple process – the cotton is thickened, stretched and strengthened until it can pass muster for weaving as either warp or weft, warp being the stronger yarn, with a higher cotton count. Ahead of us is a machine that seems to be a physical manifestation of the confusion raging through me.

The beaming machine stands tall, drawing in 504 single threads at a time on to a roll, creating a warp. It resembles a huge, diligent spider. This process can be repeated up to four times, creating rolls with 2,016 threads. Each of these warps would then be dipped into vats of starch, to strengthen them for the next step: the drawing-in. The drawer-in was a special person, quite often stone deaf from working too long in the other rooms. They worked in twos, and would sit opposite one another around their machines, staring at up at thousands of threads coming off the warp. The complexity of the task boggles the mind. They would painstakingly draw the threads, one at a time, through a seemingly impenetrable wall of mixed threads, inches from their eyes. This was done in complete silence, bent over in concentration, squinting for the next correct thread, plucking it between finger and thumb and swiftly pulling it through, collecting it. The monastic atmosphere of the drawing-in rooms must have been in stark contrast to the battlefields of the scutching and carding rooms. Thread after thread, ignoring the cramp in their unmoving legs, the dull pain behind their temples, the ache in their stiffening necks. It was surely only a matter of time before their eyesight became as poor as their hearing. Some of the finished cloths required the complexity of up to 4,000 threads. A Savile Row cloth would require up to 7,000 threads . . .

Most of the cleaning and scavenging had to be done in the precious moments that the great machines paused for mechanical breath. The spinning machines would allow their huge frames to draw out the threads on to the hundreds of spindles, then reel them back in, briefly exposing the underbelly of the frame.

In scurried the children, gathering the detritus, one eye on the returning frame, while the spinner kept his foot on a brake of sorts. The foot wouldn't be kept down for long – time was money and the overlooker would be round checking how many 'draws' the machine had been doing. Too few, or too many with imperfections, and they would be sacked. There was no room for sentiment, no room for slow children. A typical team would consist of the spinner, his assistant and a 'little piecer', a child. 'Piecing' was the act of tying together the strands of thread that had snapped, at any stage in the whole process. This was a skill many children were taught, but few were proficient enough to be allowed to piece during the spinning process. It simply wasn't an option to stop your machine to 'piece up' a broken thread. You didn't have the time. Spinners taught themselves to step into the machinery and tie up the two ends walking backwards as the frame came back at them. Then they'd have to step, just as delicately, back out into the alley in front of the machine, the ends safely pieced back together. Attentive and fleet of foot, these workers could have been a huge hit at dances, if only they'd had the time and the social standing to attend them. Having the energy for dancing would have been another problem.

A report was carried out in 1844, measuring the distance walked by a piecer over the period of one day. The resulting document was written up on 19 April. It is a meticulous piece of work, taking into account the number of 'stretches' achieved by the machine per minute: four. Then the length of each stretch: 60 inches. The length of the beam is recorded: 12 feet

4 inches. The number of steps taken by the piecer over a five-minute average: 192. The length of each step: 16 inches. Total distance: 6.9 miles. Per day. Eleven and a half hours a day. Six days a week. Nearly 42 miles a week. This would be a tough regime, even if it was to be carried out in fresh air, along country lanes with refreshment readily to hand. In the miasma of the spinning rooms and with your life at stake, it is nothing short of miraculous.

Many workers wanted to work with a crew they trusted, and so literally bred their own. Often teams were related, father and son, the son taking over the machine when his father died. The larger the family, in mill terms, the better the chance of maintaining a working life. As the business became more competitive, spinners would introduce more belts and pulleys into their machines to increase the speed and therefore increase the number of draws. No wonder they would look down on the child sprawled under the frames and count the seconds, feet twitching over the brake. The mostly male workers of all the main machinery were under constant pressure to produce, and most were too occupied even to visit the privy, preferring to piss where they stood, on to pads of raw cotton. When these were sodden, the men would signal for a child to take them away and bring a fresh wad.

It's strange that material was used in such a cavalier fashion, as waste was a major concern for the millowners, who made sure that every small scrap would be put to use. The process of fine spinning would discard some short cotton fibres. These were then mixed with some longer fibres to produce a thicker thread with little twist. This was known as condensed spinning. The waste produced from this was, in some cases, compacted into a disc shape and fed to pit ponies as 'cotton cakes'. Some of this end product was even further compacted into small bricks and were used as a cheaper alternative than coal, for very poor people in the village. There was also a machine developed to recycle used, therefore inferior, spun thread. This machine would chew up the thread until it was pulped, when it would be fed, all over again, into the scutching machine. These machines were known, appropriately, as 'devils'.

And the din must have been truly hellish. Hundreds of machines screaming together, flat out, the floors shifting and drumming with the effort, the walls shaking, windows rattling like loose teeth. The whole mill building would have come alive, pulsing with sound and fury. New apprentices staring up at it from the mill yard would have shaken in their clogs. And all the while the two waterwheels in the basement booming as the Bollin was funnelled through them, beating so fast it seemed they would tear loose from their moorings and crash through the mill walls. If the machines had not been slowly shut down at the end of every day, gradually lessening their demand for power from the mighty wheels, then the 44 tons of churning metal would simply have ripped themselves out of the basement and crashed through the mill building like so much shrapnel, and probably not stopped much short of Wilmslow itself. A sudden switching-off of the demand would have been like ramming a stout stick into the spokes of a speedily pedalled bicycle – all that energy has to go somewhere.

And the waterwheels would have had to produce even more power when weaving was introduced to the mill, after old Samuel Greg was out of the way and his son Robert Hyde could press ahead with his plans. The huge weaving looms were dragged across planking over the Bollin, and through huge holes gouged out of the mill walls. The weaving sheds had to be on the ground floor as the machines were so heavy. Once up and running, they would bring a deeper resonance to the orchestrated cacophony of the mill's music – until the looms were ripped from the mill in the 1950s. Their polished bolt ends can still be seen in the mill's restaurant, where they were sheared through.

The placing of weaving looms in the same building as the scutching, carding and spinning meant that the Gregs had a unique grip on the whole process, and the ensuing quality was outstanding. Manufacturers travelled from as far away as China to see this for themselves. But there was something of a downside. What the Gregs gained in quality and control they also unwittingly matched with aggravation. If a weaver was dissatisfied with the quality of what he was getting from the spinners, it was usually too late, the spinners often being many miles from the weavers. When they were under the same roof, it was a different story. A couple of flights of well-trodden stairs and they were face to face. The competition and rivalry were intense – livelihoods were at stake and there was no room for slacking or shoddy work.

No one would dare settle a dispute on the shop floor. Out in the woods, back in the village, or, by far the most likely, after a few pints in the Ship Inn. We know a lot of what went on from the 'Recollections' of Thomas Tonge, who worked in the mill during the 1860s, and then emigrated to America. He was in his seventies when he was tracked down, at the instigation of Lieutenant-Colonel Ernest William Greg, who was in the process of recording the history of his family's mill, and asked to set down his memories of life at Quarry Bank. Tonge mentions a Constable Joseph Bailey, dealing with yet another fight at the pub, where at times it must have felt like a wild west frontier town. More Deadwood than Styal. Bailey lived in an 'old black and white cottage', close to the inn. Probably too close for comfort. When someone ran round and tried to stir Bailey into action because two men were fighting, he was reported to have said, 'Oh, let 'em feight a bit, they'll be aisier partit.' Easier to part only after they battered themselves into submission, no matter how bad the injuries? Joseph Bailey made it through to later life as a haycutter, and it's not difficult to see how, caution always being the better part of valour in his book.

Fighting to protect your own patch can be put in context against an archived cost-assessing exercise undertaken in 1831. The Gregs set their accountants, overlookers and managers the task of discovering just how much, to a fraction of a penny, their workers were costing per pound of finished cotton produced. They started in the first card room. Here they found:

10 carders
8 drawing frame tenters
2 slubbers
4 rovers
2 creel tenters
3 odd hands
4 pepper's room

These workers resulted in: 'Production lbs. 6000 – 2 Hank Roving'. So a calculation was made: '33 Hands – Wages £9. 18s. 0½d or 0.419d per lb'.

Again, a marvellous array of evocative terms from the industrial past, some still recognised today. A slub is the dimension of cotton thickness after carding but before spinning, and the wonderfully named slubbers would have worked on this small production line. Tenters are the people who would 'camp' around a particular set or amount of machinery on a factory floor, as with the 'drawing frame tenters'. Hank roving encompasses two elements. A hank is a technical specification of cotton fibre, and a roving is a single carded, folded strand of cotton, ready for spinning. Not, as I first mooted to Chris, the name of an itinerant country and western singer. There is no mention of the apprentice children, but this doesn't mean that they fell under the radar. The cost of maintaining an apprentice system was always on the minds of the masters.

To put a human face on these statistics, the wages books record the Howlett family, those pioneers from Bledlow we met in Chapter Two, and their weekly worth to the mill:

John Howlett, employed as foreman (on the land). Aged 38	12s 0d
Mary Ann Howlett. Factory. Aged 16	4s 6d
Ann Howlett. Factory. Aged 14	3s 6d
Celia Howlett. Factory. Aged 12	2s 6d
Timothy Howlett. Factory. Aged 10	1s 6d
No younger children.	

Another migrant from Bledlow, arriving shortly after the Howletts, was a widow named Hannah Veary, with her six children. The wages book attests to the fact that all the children were put to work in the mill straightaway, on a similar scale to the Howletts:

Hannah Veary. Widow.	
Samuel Veary. Factory. Aged 18	7s 0d
Fanny Veary. Factory. Aged 18	6s 0d
Henry Veary. Factory. Aged 14	3s 6d
Joseph Veary. Factory. Aged 12	2s 1d
Mary Veary. Factory. Aged 10	1s 5d

Whereas apprentice children went unpaid, except for overtime worked at a penny an hour, the children of contracted workers like Howlett were paid a wage. This must have caused much resentment, yet held more than this one truth. Yes, apprentices went without much money, but who sat down to regular meals, often with meat at the end of every day? This was one thing the Howlett children could not count on.

Apprentices huddled together in stinking cots, but were they any worse off than the children who bedded down on cellar floors in the village? The argument ebbs and flows, but at the very least the Howlett children could boast the one thing lacking in the lives of the other apprentices. Parents.

Time and motion 1830s-style would not overlook the apprentice children, the most vulnerable of the workers. We saw earlier how it turned its hawkish glare on to measuring out medicinal powders – what would fit on a sixpence, nothing more. A trip to Manchester Central Library illuminates this penny-pinching policy.

The library holds the weekly accounts from Quarry Bank, running from September 1834 to June 1871, and are meticulously worked through. In the period from September 1834 to February 1835 the mill contained a total of 373 hands. The average weekly wage paid was 6s 5½d. The total number of spindles being used was 11,600. Average hours worked per week: 68.16. At that time there were 78 apprentices working, and the expense incurred keeping the apprentice system going was £15 14s 0d per week. During this whole period the highest number of apprentices used appears in the time between March 1838 to August 1838, when 97 boys and girls packed into the Apprentice House. This cost the Gregs £19 14s 8d per week. Everything was taken into consideration for this cost: food, clothing, medicines, educational costs, not a penny went unaccounted for. If apprentices were to be of any use, beyond the obvious one of their size, then they had to be cost-efficient.

It was during this particular period that the weaving revolution of Robert Hyde Greg got started, but the steady rise in weaving looms also coincided with the equally steady decline in the use of apprentices. At first the mill had 60 weaving looms and 97 apprentices; by 1847 it was a different story. In the period between July and December 1847, after which the apprentice system was abandoned, Quarry Bank employed 209 various millhands scutching, carding and spinning, and 180 hands in the weaving sheds. The total number of apprentices employed during this same period? Four and 'a half', which is how the Gregs would have seen a part-time person, costing them a grand total of £2 10s 0d per week. The figures for the spinning rooms and the weaving sheds remained pretty much constant for the next decade. It all went on without a single new apprentice. Those who had survived would never have to take another poor wretch under their wings. The apprentice children had fallen off the sixpence.

But while the system was in use, for more than sixty years, just how could those wretches survive this maelstrom of moving metal and this toxic cocktail they sucked into their heaving lungs? What got them through each dreaded day, what decreed that one would survive where another fell? When you cannot take one more step, lift one more finger, and your every muscle is screaming at you to stop, how do you go on? When is enough actually enough and what mortal price would you expect to pay just to come out at the end of your time in the mill in one recognisable piece?

CHAPTER FIVE

The Human Toll

The difference between life and death could be reduced to a moment's hesitation, a beat in time. As the mighty spinning machines, or 'mules' as they are known, trundle back and forth, child apprentices scuttle into the gap between them, scooping up dust and rubbish. They wriggle out again, missing the flailing metal limbs by precious seconds. But they're worked to the bone, young legs shaking with effort and bare feet trying to get purchase on the slippery, sweat-stained floor. One day it was all too much for thirteen-year-old John Foden. Maybe he couldn't think straight, maybe he was too slow . . . whatever the reason, his worst nightmare came true. His head was caught between the roller and the carriage, squashed like a ripe berry between giant fingers – 'completely smashed, death being instantaneous'. The Quarry Bank records of 6 March 1865 report this snuffing-out of a young life as 'a very melancholy accident'.

Walking around the spinning room at Quarry Bank today gives you but a fraction of the noise, none of the pollution and certainly not an iota of the danger as the machines thrash away behind the safety rail that modern Factory Acts rightly deem vital. Yet we see how remorseless and frighteningly fast those machines are. How could anybody survive their deadly embrace? While some didn't, others did, child and adult worker alike, with mixed fortunes. The archive at Quarry Bank contains logs for some of the accidents, told in sparse, cold detail.

Another young lad came all too close to ending up like John Foden. We don't know his name – the mill identifies him only as 'a boy in the mule room'. On 3 January 1889 he was under the mule 'sweeping the carriage' when he miscalculated the return of the frame, and 'finding the mule had gone too far up' had left it too late to get out. With the mule now inexorably 'in motion for another draw' his head 'was caught between the carriage and the roller beam'. Feeling the immense pressure begin to bear down on his skull, he must have believed he had drawn his final breath. Miraculously, he survived. But at a cost. The record goes on, 'the upper portion of one ear was cut off and a severe scalp wound inflicted'. After about six weeks off work, he recovered, forever carrying the healed wound as a garish reminder that time, and machines, wait for no child.

For no adult, either. Joseph Davenport, assistant to the weaving overlooker, was twenty-five years old, and by rights should have been experienced enough to keep out of trouble. However, a lot of the maintenance work needed on these machines on a daily basis involved getting as close as possible, often underneath and in between as many thrashing rows as you could fit. On 23 June 1845 Joseph was working around a loom in a weaving shed when the buckle of a strap caught on his shirt sleeve and 'snatched him up to the drum'. There it wrenched his arm off at the shoulder in front of a room full of horrified and powerless onlookers. The pressure and sheer brute power of the machine tore through muscle, sinew and flesh like so much soggy paper, exposing the bone and then snapping it as anyone would a chicken wing. We can only hope loss of consciousness was swift, as Joseph's screams must have pierced even the cacophonous din of the huge room, full of still moving machinery. The records state that he was 'immediately removed' to Manchester Infirmary – a coach ride of at least an hour, and bone-rattling at the best of times. Although he was surely given a healthy dose of laudanum before the pain-racked journey, it must have seemed to take an eternity.

There certainly would have been fellow workers watching him being loaded into the coach who doubted that they would ever see him again, and thanking God that it hadn't been them. For the child apprentices present, there could not have been a more graphic or horrific example of what the machinery could do within the beat of their hearts. Some poor souls would doubtless have been made to clean up what remained of Joseph's arm, gagging with the oily, coppery tang of his blood catching at the back of their throats as they swabbed the blood-slickened boards. Joseph was admitted to the infirmary where he died, after 'lingering' for several days.

Another worker who lost an arm was luckier. He kept his

life. The mill records tell us that on 1 April 1881 and at around three o'clock in the afternoon William Bower was working in the bottom card room. Whether the apprentices and workers in the mill ever had the time or inclination to contemplate the frivolity always associated with April Fools' Day is debatable, but for William this day couldn't have been further from a joke. The mill's official account of the accident goes on to describe how William had acted 'thoughtlessly' when going about his business in the carding room. (Though it should be remembered that accidents were often classed as being errors on the part of the person involved, with no account being taken of the conditions they worked under.) One of his duties that day was to 'press down the fly' in the box by the carding machine while cleaning it. This action usually required the pressing to be done with the use of a rod. For whatever reason – complacency, tiredness, lack of the rod itself – William fatefully pressed the fly down with his hand. What happened next is described in a plain, dispassionate fashion. William's hand was 'drawn in by the licker-in'. The damage was instant and devastating and William was transported to Stockport Infirmary as swiftly as possibly. Once there it was decided that 'the wounds were of such a nature as to render it necessary to amputate it immediately'. William seems lucky not to have bled to death, either on the journey or when the doctor's saw took off what was left of his arm.

This wasn't to be the end of William's time in employment at Quarry Bank, as the account continues: 'He recovered in the course of time and came back to work again; a mechanical arm being provided for him by the firm.' This must have been an ingenious contrivance for the time, one that the television scriptwriters picked up and adapted for the series. Though here they made it into an artificial hand, built for young Thomas Priestly by the safety-conscious engineer Daniel Bate, who also fashioned a guard for the machine.

The real Thomas didn't lose a whole hand in an accident, only a finger – though that was no doubt bad enough. We've already met him, when in 1806 he was caught as a runaway along with his friend Joseph Sefton, who gave an account of life at the mill. Thomas, born in 1793 and from Hackney in London, had a different tale to tell. Both accounts sit in the archive at Quarry Bank. Thomas tells us how he was sent from Hackney Workhouse to Styal, aged ten. After a day's rest from the long journey he was put in charge of a pair of water frames:

> My business was to supply those machines, to guide the threads occasionally and to twist when they snapt [sic]. I soon became perfect in these operations. I also learn'd to take the machines to pieces and apply the oil, a matter that required some care . . .

So, in 1803 and at a tender ten years of age, Thomas deems himself proficient at his appointed form of labour. Three years later however, it appears that he is not as perfect as he thinks.

> About two months before I left the place . . . one of the wheels caught my finger and tore it off; it was the

fore finger on my left hand. I was attended by the surgeon of the factory, Mr Holland, and in about six weeks I recovered.

Losing a finger was one of the more common injuries inflicted by machine. Another man named Bower, Christopher, lost a thumb, and could perhaps also hope for recovery – which for a while didn't seem unlikely. Aged thirty-five, he was a grinder in the carding room. He was working there on Friday 14 December 1888, cleaning the shafting of the great machines. The accretion of oil and grease in any machine was not only a fire hazard, but detrimental to the very efficiency of the machines, and stopping them for any length of time was seen as a huge waste of money. Christopher was described as 'being in the act of wiping the oil out of the grease tin', which itself was situated 'under the small pair of bevel wheels over the water wheel'. This being the wheel that would drive the frames themselves, and this time there was no instrument designed for this job, just the use of your hand. A bare description follows: 'the waste he had in his hand was caught by the wheels and his hand carried through them, mangling it in a very serious manner'. In an instant, snatched by the very teeth of the machine and chewed up like so much gristle in their daily broth. Christopher was taken to the doctor in Wilmslow, his injuries seemingly not deemed sufficiently bad to convey him to the hospital. This crucial decision was not to go in Christopher's favour.

The doctor dressed the mangled hand though 'the bleeding

continued for some time'. It then appears that Christopher, presumably filled to the brim with laudanum, returned to Quarry Bank, still bleeding. On the following Monday, after a weekend of crushing pain and prayers on Sunday, Christopher was looked at by the doctor again. This time he was sent straight to the infirmary in Stockport, where they amputated his thumb. Was this too little, too late? The report suggests 'for a short time he seemed to progress favourably'. And so Christopher spent an uncomfortable Christmas with whatever family he had, nursing his thumbless hand. Any hopes he may have harboured about returning to work and providing for this family were soon dashed. The mill record for Christopher ends abruptly: 'Later however lockjaw set in and he died on Jany. 3rd 1889.'

While Christopher was apparently convalescing, the carding room almost took another victim a week after his accident. On 22 December a lad named Peter Sprowson was attending that same carding machine, picking at a bit of cotton sticking 'between the grid and the main cylinder' when it snapped at him, sucking his fingers in, breaking one and badly 'lacerating' two others. Peter was 'attended by the factory surgeon', luckily surviving the ordeal. Still the carding machine ground on, chewing the bones and flesh of those unwary or unlucky enough to get within snatching distance, like a mad dog, snarling and snapping at them, nursing some deep grievance. The mill records this brush with death as, 'accidents like all other misfortunes "tread each others' heel" . . .' Did the hapless Peter look to the progress of his fellow worker

Christopher for signs of what was to follow for him too? If so, the third day of January and Christopher's death must have sent shivers down his spine.

As we've seen in the case of poor Joseph Davenport, the weaving sheds had their share of mishaps. Of all the accidents waiting to happen, being struck by a dislodged shuttle was the most common. If you handle a shuttle, you realise why. The sharp metal tips at either end look capable of inflicting great damage and, in some cases, death. A later account in the archives gives us an accurate insight into how this kind of accident could have occurred. A Quarry Bank document, 'I Didn't Really Have an Option: reasons for going into the mills'. contains fabulously revealing slices of mill life in the early parts of last century. One such entry recalls an incident involving a girl operating a loom next to our storyteller, simply identified as AP.

> The girl who had the looms next to me – she was a bit accident prone I must admit – and this Bob, who was our tackler at the time, he had a bit of a flare of temper and she never listened to what he said to her – and she's still the same 'cause I know her even now! And what he said to her was – well, the first time she went for him and she said, 'Look, me shuttles – there's something wrong with me shuttles', and he said, 'Alright, I'll come over,' and he was irritable. So he said switch on, and she switched on and the next thing the shuttle shot out

– and he was leaning against a wall which had a join of wood, and it shot out and pinned his overall to this piece of wood!

As if this wasn't warning enough to both Bob the tackler and the girl on the loom, moments later she called him over again. This time he wasn't going to escape so lightly.

She'd just got over that when she had to call him over again. He came over and said, 'you behave yourself with them shuttles . . . now sit there . . . and listen to me; and when I say switch on, switch on.' But I don't know whether she didn't listen to him and he's down with his hands down the side of the loom; and he said something – she thought he said switch on and being eager she jumped up and switched on! And he lost a finger! He was so angry – the language was terrible. He stood there and the blood was spurting everywhere, and he was shouting, 'Go under the loom and get me finger!' And it's rolled under the dust, and she's screaming . . . she said, 'Oh I can't, I can't!' – he said, 'Get my finger now!' In the end I had to jump off my loom and sort of scrape it out and put into a bag – somebody's lunch bag, you know, that they'd had their sandwiches in!

A colourful tale that shows us both the horror of losing a body part, albeit a minor one, and the kind of gallows humour that must have developed among the more experienced millhands. The propensity for the shuttles to fly free from their machines must have been a constant occurrence and hence a constant threat. Another millworker, recorded in 'I Didn't Really Have an Option' and identified only as GW, sheds further light: 'The only accident I had was being whacked with a shuttle right at the top of me eye . . . and that were a tackler.' Being almost wholly reliant on the expertise and attention span of your workmates was clearly part of the stress of being around the machinery. In this case GW had reason to blame his or her tackler, the person responsible for 'tackling' all the machines' niggling problems: 'He didn't stop the loom right . . . and Johnny just knocked the handle off . . .' Simple, careless mistakes made by exhausted, demoralised workers with often potentially devastating consequences. GW explains what happened to the shuttle: 'It came flying out and as I turned round it whacked me right in the corner of the eye and laid me out for a minute . . .' But GW was lucky. 'I were alright – it's knocked me a bit daft like, but . . . !'

Weaver Lucy Ramsden wasn't so lucky. On Friday 14 December 1885 a shuttle went a little closer than GW's had done. Lucy was struck in the face and was evacuated to Manchester Infirmary, where the damage was too severe to save one of her eyes. The doctors removed the eye and, after she recovered back at Quarry Bank, a replacement eye was fashioned for her out of glass. Whether she was able to remain a weaver, a good job then, especially for a woman, is not documented.

★ ★ ★

What you could never know at the time is that this seemingly simple piece of design, a shuttle, harbours a much more insidious way of killing you. As you place the new spindle of thread into it, you have to find a way of threading the loose end through a smallish hole at the end of the shuttle. With fumbling, weary fingers it's possible to steer the end into the opening of the hole, but no further. Millworkers chanced upon a simple, seemingly innocuous method of drawing the ends through. They applied their pursed lips to the end of the hole and sucked the end through into their open mouths. And so, 'kissing the shuttle' was born. This part-romantic, part-salacious act was to become an everyday, and often recurring, part of mill life, especially for the girls and women. As such, it was often remarked upon by the lads and men, not always in a complimentary manner, and usually with sexual overtones.

Kissing the shuttle had two effects, one short term, one more hidden and infinitely more deadly. Girls doing this would soon begin to notice that the staining on their teeth simply wouldn't go away. Instead, it spread until the teeth began to slowly rot, and even on the occasions when they did feel like smiling, the sudden memory of what lay behind their lips would have prevented them from doing so. It was said of Hannah Greg that she didn't smile often, especially in any portraiture, for fear of exposing her poor teeth. Hannah could point only to her squeamishness when faced with the dentist, as she never had to kiss a shuttle in her life. When you take into account what a trip to the dentist meant in the nineteenth century, you can have much sympathy for Hannah. But greater sympathy must lie with the mill girls who had more than sheer vanity to occupy themselves with. A book by D. Cameron, *A Plan and advice on cure of the Teeth* (1839) identifies treatments for toothache. These include:

Hot brandy
Oil of cloves
Opium (as laudanum)
Belladonna
Flannel dipped in brandy and sprinkled with pepper

By far the most common treatment for toothache was extraction by the use of metal pliers. Cameron does go on to describe one treatment involving the use of a heated metal wire, which was inserted into the rotten tooth as a means of extracting the 'poison'. Faced with such tortures, it is small wonder then that most chose to ignore the state of their dental hygiene until it was no longer bearable and the tooth needed to be pulled. Even these courses of treatment were mainly available only to those who could afford them, and certainly not to our mill children and workers. For the girls faced with an unruly end of thread and the furious overlooker breathing over their shoulders, kissing the shuttle was the only option – they would worry about their teeth later. When it was too late. So they would open their mouths, purse their cracked and drying lips and breathe in all those oily, clogging fibres, tasting the grease off the shuttle and then taking the toxic mix down into their lungs year after year . . .

Of course, it wasn't until medical research caught up with what the millworkers were exposed to that we can appreciate the full extent of the damage done by inhaling this deadly cocktail. When millworkers knew enough to put a name to the chronic, asthma-like narrowing of the airways, they called it 'spinner's cancer'. However, byssinosis, or brown lung disease, is not a cancer. Over time, though, it does completely steal the breath from the body and leaves the victim wheezing at every effort, chest whistling with every rise and fall. Exposure to the raw cotton was worst in the carding and scutching rooms, where the fibrous air was at its densest. These workers were expected to have the shortest working lives and the lowest life expectancy, few making it through to their forties and fifties. Children slaving here came away grey and malnourished, their young lungs blighted and failing to supply enough oxygen to the blood.

The mill's death records show the grim toll taken on apprentices, listing all those who met with early deaths between the years 1796 and 1847. The first list is of those who died of disease or ailment and had received treatment for their conditions from Dr Holland.

> Elizabeth Sutton; Died 29 September 1807, age unknown. She died of 'decline', otherwise known as tuberculosis. She appears 12 times in the medical book entries, noted as 'Betty'.
>
> Sophia Marks; Died 30 March 1815, age 21. She also

died of 'decline' and appeared 7 times in the medical book entries.

Anne Shaw; Died 13 May 1816, age 14. Her death is described as 'dropsy', probably another term for tuberculosis, and she had 16 entries in the book.

George Hodgkinson; Died 22 January 1817, age 11. George is another victim of 'decline', having appeared 6 or 7 times in the book for treatment.

John Bayley; Died February 1821, age unknown. 'Inflammation of the chest' is the stated reason for his death after 7 entries and one final one, presumably for his burial.

John J. Jackson; Died 3 March 1821, age unknown. John was a victim of smallpox and has only 2 entries before his final visit to the book.

William Wyatt; Died 16 October 1823, age 19. Again 'decline' was the cause, and poor William clocked up 25 entries before his death.

Ellen Williamson; Died 1 June 1828, age 15. 'Decline' once more, but this time Ellen must have fought hard against this wasting disease as she has the most entries for treatment, numbering 35. I'm sure, aged only 15, she must have railed against the tuberculosis, a cruel reminder of the dangers of working in such a poisonous atmosphere and its effect on the immature and over-exposed lungs of the children there.

William Metcalf; Died 5 February 1837, age 18. For the only time in the entries, 'St Vitus' Dance' is given as the reason for death. William has the only entry in the medical book for this disease, a form of rheumatic fever, cruelly named because of the jerky movements of its unfortunate victims.

Jane Skillicorn; Died 13 April 1837, age 18. After 12 entries in the book, Jane succumbed to 'decline'.

Elizabeth Grimes; Died 11 July 1838, age 15. A mystery 'stomach ailment' is given as the cause of death in Elizabeth's case, after 6 entries.

Dora Caldwell; Died 1841, age 17. Dora died following an elbow injury with ensuing infection. She made 16 entries in the medical book under her full name, Dorothy.

Finally Charlotte Watkin makes just a single entry in the medical book, on 17 June in 1811. Age unknown, she is marked as having been buried also on this day, citing 'stomach ailment'. Could she have been one girl who'd taken a terrible risk to get rid of an unwanted pregnancy? As we'll see later, there was an illicit remedy. Charlotte has no previous medical conditions and seems to have been buried in haste. To have identified 'stomach ailment' as the cause of death so quickly and then to have buried her, means that the 'ailment' was identifiable, sudden and fatal.

To complete the list of known apprentice deaths, we must add another seven names:

James Stockton; Died 25 December 1796, aged 13. The cruellest of Christmas gifts.
Mary Leather; Died age unknown in 1796.
Edwin Unwin; Died 28 July 1800, age unknown.
Thomas Podmore; Died 18 March 1803, age unknown.
Thomas Holder; Died 20 April 1828, age 11.
Elizabeth Clark; Died 15 August 1830, age 17.
Hannah Ainsworth; Died 13 April 1837, age 17.

Closer examination of the document throws up some irregularities and some explanations. William Wyatt is described as having been treated for coughs and 'oppressed breathing'. He is further described as wearing a 'flannel waistcoat' and as having been 'moved to light outdoor work'. This probably partly explains how he survived to the age of nineteen before dying of his factory-induced illnesses.

Charlotte (Kitty) Auley may be another name to add to this melancholy list. She is described as having been ill for over three years with 'severe stomach problems and a bad cough'. On 19 June 1837 she is noted as having been treated with the 'application of poultices for swelling of the legs' and 'bed rest'. Whether this sudden switch in treatment had any desired effect was never noted, for these were the final words noted in her case. After this day in June, Kitty disappears from the records.

The children and sick workers obviously received whatever treatment was deemed appropriate at the time, with the Gregs standing the cost, although this cost cannot have been too great. Most remedies, as we have seen, were natural, almost homeopathic and easily obtained (and often of doubtful efficacy). Dr Holland left a list of commands for what to do in certain cases. Given that a lot of the symptoms shown by the children were common, recurring complaints, this was a sensible and expedient practice. There was no getting over spinner's cancer, however, and although many deaths were put down to 'decline', the underlying and undeniable truth was that most victims were doomed the day they set foot inside the mill gates.

And in death, cost became a consideration. Any funeral expenses were borne by whatever money was left behind by the deceased, taken from the remains of their wages. If an adult worker died and left children who were also working at the mill, then any shortfall would be stopped from their wages. In September 1832 Hannah Ashworth buried her mother. It cost her £2 9s 7½d. At a penny an hour Hannah would have to work for nearly 600 hours before the debt was paid, if she had no savings herself.

Funerals were rudimentary. Families were invited to attend and the bodies would be taken by cart from Styal village to the church at Wilmslow, St Bart's. If the deceased had lived in the village itself, then a board could be borrowed to lay the corpse out in the family home. This board survives today, under lock and key, standing by the side of the co-op shop, a sombre reminder of past woes and familial grief.

Though to modern eyes the lot of child apprentices at Quarry Bank seems unendurably harsh, the truth is that the Gregs' regime was far and away better than most at the time. The mortality rate at Quarry Bank in fact compares very favourably with those of mills in Manchester, Lancashire and Derbyshire. These mills shared a terrible reputation. Child apprentices were treated much worse than any human would treat a dog, pig or sheep, all of which were actually more valuable – the animals literally cost more to buy than the human children. Punishment in these mills was swift and brutal and the price paid for perceived wrongdoing, or sheer idleness, was severe. In some mills, small handvices were screwed to children's noses and ears, and others favoured suspending children above working machinery. We've already heard about the brutal treatment of children in workhouses through the testimony of Robert Blincoe, recorded by journalist John Brown, and reprinted in pamphlet form in 1832 by John Doherty, the Manchester cotton-spinner's union leader. Doherty had been blacklisted by the cotton lords, being a constant thorn in their sides through his tireless campaigning against child labour and for equal rights for all men, especially working men suffering under the yoke of life in the mills. He had reinvented himself as the owner of a small coffee house and reading room and a publisher of working-class newspapers, pamphlets and books, in Withy Grove, Manchester.

By the time of the interviews with Brown, Blincoe was still inextricably tied to the cotton industry, only now he had risen above the brutality of his old daily existence and had been trying with his own small businesses, ventures that saw him in and out of jail for debt. His recollections are his own and, although bitter, he had no good reason to embellish them, and indeed, had to be tracked down and asked to recollect in the first place. Blincoe's first mill was at Lowdham in Nottinghamshire. There life was almost unbearably tough and the early promises of the parish and the mill's agents soon proved hollow. However, Blincoe survived there but when the mill closed, those apprentices with families to return to were sent back to their parishes. Foundlings like Blincoe were not, and as far as he was concerned one mill would be not too dissimilar from another. He couldn't have been more wrong. What lay ahead for him at Litton Mill in Derbyshire beggars belief. Brown offers an appalling picture.

> I have not yet done more than to mention the cuffs, kicks, or scouring, to which, in common with many of his unhappy comrades, Blincoe stood exposed, since, by his account, almost from the first hour in which he entered the Mill, till he arrived at a state of manhood, it was one continual round of cruel and arbitrary punishment. Blincoe declared, he was so frequently and immoderately beaten, it became quite familiar; and if its frequency did not extinguish the sense of feeling, it took away the terror it excited on his first entrance into this den of ignorance and crime. I asked him if he could state an average number of times in which he thought he might in safety say, he had suffered corporal punishment in a week. His answer invariably was, that his punishments were so various and so frequent, it was impossible to

> state with anything approaching to accuracy. His body was never free from contusions, and from wounds inflicted by the cruel master whom he served, by his sons, or his brutal and ferocious and merciless overlookers.

Blincoe gives Brown more specific details.

> . . . he was put to the back of a stretching frame, when he was about eleven years of age, and that often, owing to idleness, or the absence of the stretcher, he had his master's work, as well as his own to perform. The work being very coarse, the motion was rapid, and he could not keep up to the ends. For this he was sure to be unmercifully punished, although they who punished him knew the task assigned was beyond what he could perform. There were different stretchers in the mill, but, according to Blincoe's account, they were all of them base and ferocious ruffians.
>
> Robert Woodward, who had escorted the apprentices from Lowdham Mill, was considered the worst of those illiterate vulgar tyrants. If he made a kick at Blincoe, so great was his strength, it commonly lifted him off the floor. If he struck him, even a flat-handed blow, it floored him; if, with a stick, it not only bruised him, but cut his flesh. It was not enough to use his feet or his hands, but a stick, a bobby or a rope's-end. He and others used to throw rollers one after another, at the poor boy, aiming at his head, which was of course

uncovered while at work, and nothing delighted the savages more, than to see Blincoe stagger, and to see the blood gushing out in a stream!

So far were such results from deterring the monsters, that long before one wound had healed, similar acts of cruelty produced others, so that, on many occasions, his head was excoriated and bruised to a degree, that rendered him offensive to himself and others, and so intolerably painful, as to deprive him of rest at night, however weary he might be. In consequence of such wounds, his head was over-run by vermin. Being reduced to this deplorable state, some brute of a quack doctor used to apply a pitch cap, or plaster to his head. After it had been on a given time, and when its adhesion was supposed to be complete, the terrible doctor used to lay forcibly hold of one corner and tear the whole scalp off his head at once. This was the common remedy; I should not exaggerate the agonies it occasioned, were I to affirm, that it must be equal to anything inflicted by the American savages, on helpless prisoners, with their scalping knives and tomahawks.

The occasionally florid language and prose style of Brown's writing should not detract from the very real horror suffered by Blincoe. This was nothing less than systematic abuse, a dehumanising force of will that must have been prevalent in most of the mills of the time. Worse was to come for Blincoe.

> This same ruffian [Robert Woodward] who, by the concurrent testimony of many sufferers, stands depicted, as possessing that innate love of cruelty which marked a Nero, a Caligula, or a Robespierre, used, when Blincoe could not, or did not keep pace with the machinery, to tie him by the wrists to a cross beam and keep him suspended over the machinery till his agony was extreme. To avoid the machinery, he had to draw up his legs every time it came out or returned. If he did not lift them up, he was cruelly beaten over the shins, which were bare; nor was he released, till growing black in the face, and his head falling over his shoulder, the wretch thought his victim was near expiring. Then after some gratuitous knocks and cuffs, he was released and instantly driven to his toil, and forced to commence, with every appearance of strength and vigour, though he were so much crippled, as to be scarcely able to stand.

Perhaps most awful of all was the fact that men like Woodward had been apprentices themselves, becoming the very worst kind of poacher-turned-gamekeeper. Having suffered conditions and treatment like this themselves, instead of choosing to try and alleviate the suffering of the poor children in their care, they seem to gain satisfaction in making their miserable lives so much worse. It is a damning indictment of certain types of human nature that people will always, it seems, be capable of inflicting pain and atrocities on their fellow human beings without remorse and with some degree of perverse pleasure.

The overlookers at Litton seemed hell-bent on outdoing each other in their wickedness. Blincoe recalls an episode that nearly saw him go the way of Quarry Bank's John Foden.

> Woodward has often insisted upon Blincoe cleaning all the cotton away under the whole frame, in a single draw, and to go out at the further end, upon pain of a severe beating. On one of these occasions, Blincoe had nearly lost his life, being caught between the faller and the head piece, his head was jammed between them. Both his temples were cut open and the blood poured down each side of his face, the marks to be seen. It was considered next to a miracle, that he escaped with his life. So far from feeling the least compassion, Woodward beat him cruelly, because he had not made *more* haste! Blincoe says, to the best of his recollection, he was twelve years of age when this accident happened.

To emphasise the climate of competition between the overlookers, Brown relates more horrors.

> There seemed to exist a spirit of emulation, and infernal spirit, it might with justice be designated, among the overlookers of Litton Mill, of inventing and inflicting the most novel and singular punishments. For the sake of being the better able, and more effectually to torment their victims, the overlookers allowed their thumb and fore-finger nails to grow to an extreme length, in order

> that, when they *pinched their ears*, they might make their nails meet [marks still to be seen.]

The overlooker Woodward exhibited the kind of malignant behaviour that wouldn't have been out of place in the Nazi concentration camps, latter-day Iraqi torture chambers or the ethnic cleansing of recent history in central Europe. Places and times where monstrous men acted with seeming impunity when treating fellow humans with a flagrant disregard for their very humanity. Witness another act of barbarism dressed as a favourite pastime for the overlookers of Litton Mill:

> Another of these diabolical amusements consisted in filing the apprentices' teeth! Blincoe was once constrained to open his mouth to receive this punishment, and Robert Woodward applied the file with great vigour. Having punished him as much as he pleased, the brute said with a sneer, 'I do this to sharpen thy teeth, that thou may'st eat thy Sunday dinner the better.'

To have fallen prey to these devilish men, prowling the mill floors with their long nails, tooth files and nobby sticks must have demoralised the children to such a degree that many must have felt they somehow were deserving of this fate. In the way many contemporary victims of abuse are told that it is their fault the abuse continues, then so must the mill children have fallen in with this doctrine.

It is worth examining the differing reactions of those

interviewed about their time in the mills. Blincoe's account was unwavering, visceral and detailed. He mentions a fellow worker called 'Blackey', whose suffering, if it was possible, seems worse than Blincoe's.

> Among Blincoe's comrades in affliction, was an orphan boy, who came from St. Pancras workhouse, whose proper name was James Nottingham; but better known as '*Blackey*', a nickname that was given to him on account of his black hair, eyes, and complexion.
>
> According to Blincoe's testimony, this poor boy suffered even greater cruelties, than fell to his own share, by an innumerable number of blows, chiefly inflicted on his head; by wounds and contusions, his head swelled enormously, and he became stupid. To use Blincoe's significant expression, 'his head was as soft as a boiled turnip', the scalp on the crown pitting ever where on the least compression. This poor boy, being reduced to this most pitiable condition, by unrestrained cruelty, was exposed to innumerable outrages, and was, at last, incapable of work, and often plundered of his food; melancholy and weeping, he used to creep into holes and corners, to avoid his tormentors. From mere debility, he was inflicted by incontinency of stools and urine.

Brown received word that James Nottingham was still working in a mill, and set about tracking the unfortunate lad down, with mixed results.

> Having learnt, in 1822, that this forlorn child of misery was then at work in a cotton factory, near Oldfield Lane, I went in search of him and found him. At first, he seemed much embarrassed, and when I made enquiries as to his treatment at Litton Mill, to my surprise he told me, he 'knew nothing about it'. I then related what Blincoe and others had named to me, of the horrid tortures he endured.
>
> 'I dare say,' said he, mildly, 'he told you the truth, but I have no distinct recollections of anything that happened to me during the greater part of the time I was there. I believe,' said he, 'my suffering was most dreadful, and that I nearly lost my senses.'
>
> From his appearance, I guessed he had not been so severely worked as others of the poor crippled children whom I had seen. As well as I can recollect, his knees were not deformed, or, if at all, but very little. He is much below the middle size as to stature. His countenance round, and his small and regular features bore the character of former sufferings and present tranquillity of mind.

Was this the state of 'beguiling slavery' Frederick Engels found at Quarry Bank? A state where individuals, so beaten down, would not dare betray their abusers for fear of the terrible consequences? Blincoe spoke as a free man, free from reprisals, that is. James Nottingham spoke as a man still fearful of a beating, or perhaps as one who had not completely 'nearly

The Apprentice House as it appears today. Inside it has been restored to how it would have looked in the nineteenth century and visitors can get a real sense of what life would have been like for the apprentice children living there, sometimes numbering as many as a hundred.

In 1847, after the abandonment of the apprentice system, the Apprentice House became a private residence for the manager and was also used as a laundry.

Boy apprentices from the television series. They sit in the simple wooden cots that were used in all the dorms and where the real apprentice children would have slept, at least two to a cot.

The real Susanna Catterall, here portrayed by Holly Lucas, was the only apprentice whom the records show taking a pregnancy to full term and returning to work in the mill.

A defiant Esther Price as played by actress Kerrie Hayes. Esther was the most famous of all the apprentice children, causing no end of trouble for the Gregs. In the television series, she is portrayed as a spirited, determined Liverpudlian.

The real Lucy Garner was Esther Price's partner-in-crime and fled to Liverpool with her, sparking one of the mill's most notorious stories. Here, Lucy is played by Katherine Rose Morley.

Esther, shorn of her hair, after her escape to Liverpool and her fateful night with the corpse of her recently deceased stewardess.

Sacha Parkinson plays Miriam Catterall, fictional sister to Susanna and victim of sexual abuse in series one of *The Mill.*

The real Mary Bowden. This is the only surviving picture of an apprentice. Mary died in 1877 from 'chronic bronchitis exhaustion' aged fifty-four and just one year after this was taken.

Claire Rushbrook plays Mrs Timperley, here doling out the lunchtime porridge and not long for this world. Her death sparked a series of events that rocked the real world of the mill and Quarry Bank.

Kevin McNally plays Mr Timperley. Deemed as unfit for purpose by the real Robert Hyde Greg, Mr Timperley nearly played a disastrous role in the history of the Apprentice House.

Overseer Charlie Crout, played by Craig Parkinson. In the fiction, a monster threatening the apprentices under his charge; in reality a romantic man with a doomed marriage.

Matthew McNulty plays Daniel Bate, the series' engineer and people's champion. The real Daniel arrived at Quarry Bank long before the time of the series, but was indeed an engineer sprung from debtor's jail by the Gregs.

The real Dr Peter Holland, medical pioneer, friend to the Gregs and uncle to Elizabeth Gaskell. He would have been one of the first people many of the apprentices met on arrival at the mill.

John Howlett (here played by Mark Frost) came from the poorest and filthiest of hovels in the Midlands, dressed in rags, and thrust his children into the mill. The second television series sees Howlett clashing fiercely with Esther and Daniel.

Mill workers pictured in March 1892. This photograph shows two members of the Venables family: Henry, second from the left, and John, far right. Second in from the right is Jonathan Davenport. The Venables and Davenport families are inextricably woven into the fabric of Quarry Bank's history.

Above: The old stag at bay, Donald Sumpter plays Samuel Greg in his dwindling twilight years. Proud to the last, yet beset by doubt and prevarication, resisting pressure from his sons to modernise the mill and secure its future.

Inset: Portrait of the real Samuel Greg, ironic smile in place and with just a hint of that famous twinkle. At the height of his powers.

Opposite top: Hannah Greg adored her gardens and the landscape of her domain. Here actress Barbara Marten portrays her in old age, greatly troubled by the slaving past of her husband's family.

Inset: Portrait of the real Hannah Greg, clearly from her time at Quarry Bank and with her mouth firmly closed, hiding the teeth she couldn't bear to show to the dentist.

Opposite: Jamie Draven plays the progressive Robert Hyde Greg. The real Robert Hyde pressed ahead with plans that eventually meant that today we can still wander around the mill. A sometimes cold and unresponsive man, he was also capable of fierce love and blessed with tremendous foresight.

Inset: Photographic portrait of Robert Hyde Greg when he was master of Quarry Bank Mill.

Quarry Bank Mill today, as seen from the path above that weaves down from the National Trust car park. Hidden in the trees is the only road in and out of the mill itself. Did this once carry the recently stolen wages in the dead of that famously stormy night?

The contradiction that is Quarry Bank Mill. A beautiful setting or a monstrous building. This is the bridge separating the mill from Quarry Bank House and was possibly the last thing William Potts saw as he disappeared under it. This photograph was taken by the final Greg to own Quarry Bank, Colonel Alec Greg.

lost his senses' as he admitted, but had lost enough of them not to know the difference any more.

You come away from reading this feeling that any child in Litton's mills and the like would have fallen into Quarry Bank thinking they'd arrived in heaven. Not only were you not beaten, but, if and when injured, you were cared for and often kept on until your injuries had healed . . . or you died, in which case you were past caring anyway. If people are treated worse than animals then eventually they come to expect nothing less and accept their lot. At Quarry Bank, even though most were probably unaware it existed, there was always a kind of hope. A cruel kind of hope if it was always out of your reach, but there nonetheless. The Greg policy of not beating their child workers seems, on the face of it, empathetic and kindly. However, it made business sense too. A beaten and injured child would do less and less work until they were worthless to the millowner. Far better to fine them for any perceived weakness, lack of application, effort or misdemeanour. In this way the workers were always tied to the mill, forever paying off fines, needing to put in that overtime just to try and keep even. Altruism with a price tag.

Not that this approach would have cut any ice with the political activist John Doherty. The righteous anger he and other liberal thinkers must have felt when confronted with stories like Blincoe's surely fuelled the furnace of their ceaseless campaigning, and no amount of protestations of innocence from the Gregs would have placated him. All child labour was slave labour, irrespective of how you treated them. Degrees of evil did not detract from the very nature of the act.

Nobody asked the children, of course. Whether they themselves would have preferred a bearable beating that was soon over to a long-drawn-out financial penalty can only be guessed at. They had no choice anyway. Unless of course it was the ultimate and most desperate choice: to run away.

CHAPTER SIX

Running Away

Everyone has a breaking point. Something tips them, senses and emotions out of kilter, into an abyss of despair. Some will rally, some will fall, never to get up again. Some rail against the unjustness of it all and fight back the only way they know how: by rebelling. And at Quarry Bank there was a way you could perform the ultimate act of rebellion and over a hundred desperate children did just that. The runaways of Quarry Bank Mill.

Not everyone from this angry, bitter group of children ran away as soon as they could, and not all ran away fuelled by that feeling of injustice. Some were simply homesick. Esther Price took until 1836, three years after her indenture, to flee back to Liverpool with Lucy Garner in tow, and we will later examine the fallout from her escape. The television series shows her leaving an uncertain Lucy outside the gates to Liverpool Workhouse, and then being hoodwinked by a churchman, the very person, who had promised to help her. And all this sandwiched between an almost casual, accidental bout of prostitution on her part, driven by hunger and a need to stay somewhere safe. With the exception of the selling of her body, this speculation is probably accurate. In the show it is the threatening form of Apprentice House steward, Mr Timperley, who recaptures the girls and returns them to Quarry Bank. The same fictional Timperley who abandons young Catherine to die of exposure so that he can spend the rescue expenses on a good steak. The decent steak certainly does seem to have been part of the 'perks' of setting out on such a mission.

One record of such a mission appears in the mill's accounts. The document is signed and dated 31 May 1841 by John Waterworth. Waterworth was an ex-apprentice-turned-bookkeeper who often worked with his two sons. He appears to have been somewhat self-important, clearly believing himself to have risen successfully from his low birth, or at least from the circumstances which saw him apprenticed in the first place. We have a record of him from the 'Recollections' of Thomas Tonge, that valuable source of information. Tonge recalls Waterworth as 'a round, fat, oily man of God'. He goes on to describe how, after his death, his wife lived on in the village of Styal, calling herself 'Lady Waterworth'. It's not recorded if Waterworth went after Esther and Lucy himself, but he certainly tracked down two other Liverpool lasses. Eliza Huddleston and Betty Wallis chose the spring of 1841 to take flight, with Waterworth hot in pursuit. His expenses form tells us the rest of the story:

> Expenses to collect and escort Eliza Huddleston and Betty Wallis from Liverpool to QBM.

Expenses to Manchester by Railway	1s 3d
Expenses from Manchester to Liverpool by Railway	6s -
Dinners, teas, supper, Bed & Breakfast at Liverpool	6s 9d
Expenses on returning from Liverpool by railway	13s 6d
From Manchester to Altrincham by boat	1s 6d
	£1 9s 0d
½ the above expenses to B Wallis	14s 6d
½ the above expenses to E Huddlestone	14s 6d

So the girls shared the cost of Waterworth's little excursion to Liverpool, probably without getting the merest sniff of the food they'd paid for. Fourteen shillings and sixpence is a lot of overtime.

Taking Esther's explosive character into account, the matter of flight was also just a matter of time. Job Baker was different. We have already tracked Job's early days at Quarry Bank and read what a compliant, earnest boy he was. In R. Murray's *Reply to Robert Blincoe* Job describes how well he was treated. After taking his interviewer through the initially gruelling workload, Job expands his descriptions to include the larger world around the factory floors and is respectful when considering his treatment. Even in illness Job felt cared-for, respected:

> On one occasion when he was confined to bed, Mrs Greg came up to the 'prentice house with some slices of

chicken and, a great luxury, a mug of tea. Her daughters would also visit any apprentices who were sick while her sons, when they came home on vacation from the University, used to give lectures at the debating society which the children and the older men attended once a week.

None of this contradicts what we know of the Gregs' behaviour from many other sources. So, if Job felt so looked-after, so secure and encouraged, then why did he run away? We know that, when he arrived at Quarry Bank, he joined his older sister, Mary, who'd held the young Job's hand, and we feel sure that Job was pleased to find her there. After all, she and younger brother George were all the family he had left in the world. So he surely must have eagerly anticipated the arrival of George into the mill, the full family house, so to speak. George arrived later, having lived his first few formative years in the workhouse at Congleton. Whereas Job had at least some memories of his parents, and Mary had more, George had none. All he knew was workhouse life, most of it without his siblings. It wasn't long before George was in trouble. There are differing accounts of his misdemeanours, but all seem to point up the actions and behaviour of a bad 'un. Even the slightly sugar-coated *Reply to Robert Blincoe* tells it straight: 'He broke a window in the master's house and was fined eight shillings.' Soon afterwards he was caught stealing apples in the village, and this was a serious crime in the eyes of Samuel Greg. He did not mind the apprentices having apples from his own garden but was very jealous of his reputation in the district of his mill and its workpeople. For this crime George was fined five shillings. He upped the ante every time he misbehaved. He'd stolen, he'd smashed the master's windows, what next? How did Job and Mary take to this behaviour? Did they envy young George his determination? Or did they curse his stupidity and hope they weren't tarred with the same brush?

Job's reaction to George's wilfulness proved extreme. While in the midst of his brother's mischief-making days at the mill, Job suddenly woke up one day and decided he'd had enough. It must have been a spur-of-the-moment decision because he left behind the wages he'd earned during his apprenticeship. It was no small amount and attested to the good work and the many sixpences he must have accrued over his time there. The stoppages ledger for 26 April 1827 reads, 'Ran away, balance forfeited, £4 1s 0d'.

He could have spent this on any number of items, especially, if he was planning on doing a runner, some new shoes. Why leave all this behind, when he'd been doing so well? Why split up his family all over again? He was only fourteen years old, what could he hope to achieve out there in the big, wide world? Perhaps that was what drove him, a sense of adventure? Maybe seeing his wild younger brother strain at the very shackles that bound him to the mill sparked something in Job. Maybe he, Mary and George had discussed running away? Job had seemed cowed by what he encountered at Quarry Bank, and who would condemn him for that? He'd already shown an interest in the outside world, taking trips out to visit Lacey

Green and Broadheath. He'd sat and listened to those tales of the pack-horse men, carrying salt from Northwich, and heard those yarns about the campaigns of the great Duke of Wellington. He'd seen the Bridgewater Canal stretching off into the distance towards Liverpool. He'd doubtless heard night-time tales about Liverpool itself from fellow apprentices, about the docks, the great ships, the smells, the dangers, the excitement. Did he seek out an adventure for himself? Whatever the reason, that late April day saw Job melt away from Quarry Bank, leaving his siblings behind.

The George that remained was no less troublesome and, it seemed, no less inclined to stay enslaved to the machines. In 1829 George took his older brother's lead and fled. Perhaps this had been the plan all along, that George would follow when he was old enough and maybe Mary as well? It didn't work, as George didn't get far. Once recaptured and returned, the Gregs decided they'd had enough. George was sent to prison. He was thirteen years old. And he was charged for the pleasure. The stoppages ledger against his name reads, '9th February 1829 – For apprehending to prison, £1 9 shillings'.

Either what happened to George while he was in prison changed him, or he simply exorcised whatever demons he'd brought from the workhouse, because, once he was safely back in Styal, one story goes that he never committed another crime and remained there for the rest of his days. As is often the case with history, there is another version of George's subsequent fortunes. This version goes that he was never heard of again, for there is no statistical evidence he ever returned. Reformists at the time preferred the former version and would have loved the idea that a young tearaway, with little or no regard for the law and its consequences, underwent a complete transformation after a spell behind bars. The 'Job Baker vs Robert Blincoe' stance had become a politically hot potato and rumours could well have been circulated to the effect that George had mended his ways and become a model citizen and worker. The *Reply to Robert Blincoe* states that Job was never heard of again. However, a Job Baker does appear again. This one appears in the 1851 census, listed as being thirty-nine years old and living as a lodger in Navigation Road, Burslem. The name, age and the location fit. Whatever Job had got up to in the meantime, it seems he had returned home.

Records show that of the hundred-plus apprenticed children who ran away between the years 1785 to 1847, at least thirty of them were never heard of again. The earliest escapees appear in the mill's cash book:

> October 20th, 1788 James Stothard's expenses in search of lads eloped . . . 2s 6d
> November 7th, 1788 Total expenses for committing 2 lads to prison for elopement . . . 15s
> April 16th, 1789 To advertisements for lads eloped . . . 2s 6d
> December 5th, 1789 Sundry expenses for lads eloped . . . £1 0s 0d

These lads remained anonymous, although those in the final entry on the list, escaping on 5 December 1789, must have achieved some distance to run up a cost of one whole pound. The first named runaway is John Yates, appearing in the apprentice wages book of 1790. He was fourteen and left his ten-year-old sister, Ann, behind in the mill. John made a break for it in 1792, was caught in Middlewich, and ran off again in 1797. This time he was not for catching; he disappears from the records.

Some apprentices fled just the once. They either succeeded in escaping capture, never to surface again, or were returned, caved in and succumbed to the monotonous, dangerous life that seemed fated for them. Some gave it one or two goes before admitting defeat. Some were serial absconders, the 'cooler kings' of Quarry Bank Mill. First out of the blocks in the serial runaway stakes was John Wright. John first ran away on 12 October 1802. He was back the next day. He waited nine months. On 27 June 1803 he ran away for a second time. Nearly a year wiser, he must have chosen a different route for he managed almost two weeks of freedom. He was back at the mill by 9 July. For his final attempt, John must have worked things out in his mind, bided his time, determined not to make the same mistakes again. Two years later and on 9 June, he was off once more. How long did he have the scent of freedom in his nostrils? Sadly, for John, just four days. On the 13th he was back and there were no more entries for him. Maybe he'd tried three different routes of escape and decided that none of them had worked successfully for him, escape was impossible and further attempts, therefore, futile?

John was determined and seemingly patient in his attempts. The same could not be said of anyone at the mill with the name Tittensor. There were three lads with this name recorded at Quarry Bank, all from Newcastle, Staffordshire, and all surely brothers. They carried out a concerted campaign of desertion, all kicked off by Edward Tittensor, aged ten years, on 20 June 1802. By 7 July, he was back. Hardly pausing for breath, on 18 July Edward took off again. This time he was on the run for almost a month, before being captured and returned on 17 August.Then, as if passing an absconder's baton, his brother John disappeared from the mill on 26 September, almost a month to the day of Edward's return. John really was gone, though, leaving 'no trace'.

Enter William Tittensor, who seemed destined to outshine his brothers. William begins his own personal campaign on 3 June 1803. He remains free for just one day, being returned on the 4th. On 4 September that year, he tries again. He manages two days this time, being returned on 6 September. He waits through a whole winter before trying again. On 30 May 1804, William's out of the doors and away – but it seems he's allowed himself to become rusty over the winter and he's captured and returned that same day. This failure seems to have a sobering, demoralising effect on young William, for it takes him almost eighteen months before he tries again. Then, on 8 December 1805, he makes another break for it. Frustratingly, he only manages two days on the road, but then again, it is winter and he'd have had to have been sleeping rough. On 10 December he's back in the Apprentice House. Clearly now, even William is slowing down. His next entry is nearly two and a half years later, on 20 March 1808. Interestingly, there is no date written down for his return, but returned he was, because in July 1809 he makes his final break for freedom, on 16 July. Did William's pig-headed, never-say-die attitude stand him in good stead for life outside the mill? There is a final entry in the mill records, which reads that on 7 October 1809, William Tittensor enlisted as a soldier. Well, that was one way of ensuring that you stayed out of the mill. Let us hope that he was never engaged as a scout.

Given that William had difficulty staying free while navigating the lanes and byways around Wilmslow, he'd have had no chance doing what the next two runaways managed. Less of an absconding, more of an odyssey. Thomas Priestly and Joseph Sefton are probably the most famous of the absconders from Quarry Bank. This isn't just because their testimony was taken by the magistrates in Middlesex and published as a matter of record, as we have seen. It is also because they walked all the way to London. Thomas Priestly is the poor lad who lost a finger and, recuperating, 'thought of his mother'. Thomas went on to describe how he and Joseph set about their quest. Thomas clearly contacted his mother; she was probably made aware he'd lost a finger. 'She sent me a crown, so I set off with Joseph Sefton.' That simple. Mrs Priestly, down in London, must have known why she was sending the crown to her son and must have known what would happen afterwards, but she too, desperately wanted to see her maimed son. Joseph also wanted his mother, as he told the magistrates: 'With respect to my coming away I wished to see my mother. I had asked leave to be absent for a month of my Master Mr Greg and he refused me so I set off without his consent with Thos Priestly about 6 weeks ago.'

Joseph was to become known as 'the boy who asked for a holiday'. This event seems to have created a lot of fuss, but, like all absconding apprentices, the boys had broken the terms of their indenture, they had broken a legally binding contract. Never mind that most had simply been shown where to put their 'mark', usually a cross, on to a piece of paper they had little or no chance of understanding. Never mind that they had even less choice in the matter. They were bound.

Joseph drew on his independent means: 'I had a shilling when we set out we slept in barns and did not spend more than 2d or 3d a day each. The shilling I had arose from my overwork.' So with six shillings between them, and only a rudimentary idea of where exactly they were and in which direction they needed to take, off they went. Roads in 1806 were rough, unmade tracks mostly and travellers often fell prey to the many footpads, cutpurses and highwaymen travelling their lengths, looking for people to rob. The penalty for highway robbery was death, so these were desperate men. Even footpads were either thrown straight into jail or deported. The two teenagers – Thomas was thirteen and Joseph seventeen – must have often been afraid for their lives. Travel by day and by the main roads and take the chance of being spotted and caught. Travel in the dark and tremble at every shift in the shadows, their breaths catching in their chests. They must have scurried from barn to barn, occasionally stopping to ask directions with whatever story they had concocted to cover their flight. Joseph tells us that the whole journey took them around six weeks, which means they averaged around forty to forty-five miles per week. Still, they had each other, it was June and so the days were long and, hopefully, the weather kind. They would have fallen asleep each night with the sickly-sweet scent of the cooling hay beneath their backs, high up on top of the bales, out of sight and looking down on the countryside. They'd have awoken to birdsong and the dawning of the day and climbed down silently so as not to alert the farmer, then just as silently drifted away, shaking the stiffness from their young legs. Then, later, once the sun had sunk down from the afternoon's glare and begun to bleed yellow and red all over the landscape, they'd have sought another farm. And waited, probably for cover of darkness and the last glimpse of the farmer or his dog, then crept over to the barn and hauled themselves up, back into a new sanctuary and the promise of a safe night's sleep. Night after night, for six weeks, until that first triumphant sight of the sprawl of London, and their waiting mothers.

Only one lad knew his father, although they had similar accounts of their humble beginnings. Joseph stated, 'My Father, I am informed, deserted me or went for a soldier, when I was about 2 years old. His name was John Sefton. I have been told that I was born at Clerkenwell. I have been in the workhouse of the Parish of Hackney from an infant.'

Thomas tells the magistrates, 'I was born as I am informed by my mother near Gray's Inn Lane. I am 13 years of age, I have no father, he has been dead for more than 2 years, he was one of the Turnkeys at Newgate. I have been informed that for about 5 years since I was taken to Hackney Workhouse.'

It is a telling feature of these transcriptions and of the stories of most of these apprentices' lives, that few knew their true ages, and if they did at some point in their infancy, they soon lost track. Without a parent to know the details and without the family around to remind them, the years slipped by without meaning, each grinding day blending into another, until all time melded into a seamless stream of monotony, punctuated by the occasional act of extreme mechanical violence. At least Thomas and Joseph had done the unthinkable and made it to London, back to their mothers, to know that feeling again, to feel their mothers' arms around them again, even if it was probably for the last time. Thomas ends his account, 'I have been in town 5 weeks in Hackney Workhouse and am very willing to go back again.'

Although it seems both boys returned willingly, there are no further records of their time back at Quarry Bank. Perhaps they simply took up where they left off, leading blameless lives and keeping well under the overlookers' radar. Their full rehabilitation would have been an industrial feather in the Gregs' cap, and no one would have blamed them for holding these two lads up as examples of how Quarry Bank wasn't such a bad place after all. But, then again, the Gregs had never been in the habit of shouting from the rooftops about their employees. They would respond robustly to defend any attack, like the frequent comments by John Doherty, but on the whole preferred to keep their counsel when it came to apprentices. However, the fact that neither lad ever appears in any record, even the wages books that survived, is strange. It could be that those records pertaining to Joseph and Thomas simply disappeared, or it could be that the lads themselves also disappeared. They'd done it once, why not again? Would the Gregs go to the trouble of attracting more attention to the flight of their apprentices? We will never know, although it wouldn't have been the first time an apprentice was given the benefit of the doubt, only to have the masters' trust shoved back in their faces.

Joseph Stockton was apprenticed in 1796, for the next eight years of his life. His age is not stated, but to be apprenticed for eight years could have taken him up to his eighteenth birthday, making him ten years old. Three years into his indenture, on 10 March 1796, Joseph was allowed home to Newcastle-under-Lyme for a week. This was not unheard of, young apprentices being allowed back with whatever remained of their families, for a kind of compassionate leave. When Joseph had not returned by 6 June, a warrant was issued for his arrest. He was duly found and returned on the 19th. Joseph was put straight back into work but obviously had no intention of sticking around. The very next day he was off again, probably waiting until he'd been roused from his cot, and set off as the sun rose, down the cobbled road to the mill. Then he'd have peeled away from his fellow apprentices, probably asking them not to split on him, and he was away, across the fields, Newcastle bound. Unfortunately for Joseph, one of the first people he ran into, having attained the outskirts of his home town, was the constable. What were the chances, especially as his face must have still been fresh in the constable's mind? He was turned on his heels and marched back to Quarry Bank. On 13 June a contrite Joseph spoke to his masters and 'promised to mind his business and give us no further trouble in future and was set back to work'. This must have sounded and seemed sincere, for Joseph was back under the yoke for the rest of the month and, to be fair to him, most of July. Had he lured his masters into a false sense of security, and been biding his time? It seems so, for, on 22 July 1799, Joseph ran away yet again. This time, however, he must have successfully avoided the constable and indeed anyone else looking for him because Joseph Stockton was never heard of again. I suppose, in one sense, he was true to his word. He never did trouble them again, in the whole of his future.

The problem of what to do if you were desperate to run away – and desperate you must have been – and you had a younger sibling with you, did not seem to put a stop to the determination of the aforementioned Tittensor brothers. Maybe they figured that travelling alone gave them a better chance of avoiding recapture? Presumably tracking down three brothers, probably not looking totally dissimilar, would have made detection easier. So when the Kettle lads from Newcastle, Staffordshire, planned a getaway, did one plead to be taken with his older brother? It would have been a painful decision to have left one behind, but perhaps they were so close that this was never an option? It could have been that a dying or desperate parent, on giving the boys up to the mill, had made the elder promise always to look after the younger. So, on 4 July 1803, both Kettle boys turned their backs on Quarry Bank and fled. They didn't remain free for long, and they didn't stick together either. Maybe the younger brother had lagged behind? Was he too weakened by his toil in the mill to make the distance needed? Did the brothers sit down one night and have a terrible conversation, deciding that one must plough on ahead, leaving the other to fend for himself? Or was it much more simple than that, and considerably less emotionally painful? It is entirely possible that the boys were surprised by someone, maybe even that eagle-eyed constable who could well have been patrolling his district only four years later. In their panic, the stronger and faster could well have escaped whilst the other struggled in the unforgiving arms of his captor. Whatever the scenario regarding his return, Peter Kettle, aged ten years, was back at Quarry Bank a week later. Joseph Kettle, aged fifteen, avoided the long arm of the law for another five days. Perhaps he made his way back to a parent who upbraided him for leaving his brother behind and was shamed into giving himself up? Maybe he did his level best to stay free, agonising over Peter's fate but not being able to do anything about it until he suffered the same? Maybe he was so incensed that he took a few days to decide to do something about it?

Once back at Styal, the Kettle lads had a chance to go over

everything in their minds. And one thing on their minds was escaping again. Only now something had changed. Either this salutary experience affected one of the boys so much they couldn't bear to go through it again, or a huge, life-changing row ensued between the two. Whatever exchange passed between the Kettle boys, on 24 July there was another breakout. Only this time Joseph was alone, and he never came back. Did Peter watch his brother run, across those fields again, never looking back? Was there a single beat of his heart when he almost took flight himself, calling for his brother to wait? Whatever raced through Peter's thoughts, he must have turned his head away and shuffled off to the mill, joining the others, making sure he wasn't late and locked out. That night, back in his half-empty cot, did he secretly pray for his brother's safe return to the Apprentice House or did he wish him Godspeed? The overlookers and stewards must have kept a sharp eye on young Peter for a few weeks after that.

Then we must consider the well-documented case of Esther Price and Lucy Garner. Esther, like Thomas Priestly and Joseph Sefton, attracted the attention of the magistrates, but not for the running away, mainly for the treatment of her on her return. Esther and Lucy made off on 27 August 1836. Lucy, we know, was returned just four days later while Esther remained at large until 5 September. What happened after changed her life forever and is dealt with in the next chapter. It would seem that whatever the true reason for Esther to run away (she said it was for an 'extended' holiday), she never tried it again. Perhaps, with regard to her changed circumstances and the revelation of her real age, she never needed to? Their flight, like that of the boys to London, must have made for a picaresque journey. In the television series we see them cheekily hijacking Timperley's cart while he's looking for them in the woods – which is entirely in character. One thing we know for sure is that the girls also took off in summer with the benefit of those longer days and warmer nights. Maybe they followed the renowned Bridgewater canal, knowing it would lead them directly to Liverpool, and maybe they did hitch a lift off a passing barge? I can imagine Esther wanting to travel home in some style. Walking? That would have been for lesser mortals. She almost certainly came back to Quarry Bank via the train and with a very watchful eye being kept on her.

Girls didn't always run away in pairs. Some bolted alone. Up to the year 1803, all the named runaways were boys. Then on 12 June that year, something happened to one girl that made her pluck up her courage and take to her heels. Hannah Jackson of Newcastle, Staffordshire, ran away twice in the summer of 1803, a popular year for legging it, eventually returning on 9 July and staying put thereafter. Four years later, on 12 July 1807, Elizabeth Wright of Nantwich followed suit. She managed to avoid capture for ten whole days, plenty of time to make it to Nantwich and see whoever she had set out to see again, before being spotted and returned. Another four years down the line and it was the turn of Ellen Steel of Newcastle, Staffordshire (again). Ellen tried twice, first on 2 March 1811, managing four days initially. She was off again in May, this time being away for only two days. After that she didn't bother and stayed put.

Many entries in the stoppages ledger just have the legend 'cash or money forfeited' written against a name. The assumption was, and still is, that no one would readily forfeit hard-earned cash for any other reason than that they absconded, not being able to claim it before they fled. Any moneys owing to the apprentices could be accessed only on demand, or rather, on request. The apprentice had to have a good reason for any expenditure and planning to run away wasn't one of them. There seem to have been an awful lot of slippers bought around this time, mostly by girls, and I have often wondered if any smart lass took the money out with no intention of splashing out on footwear, but with flight on her mind. Then, perhaps passing the shop window in the village, she spotted the slippers in question and reconsidered her situation. Wouldn't any reasonable person, thinking of fleeing, set out first to ensure they at least had decent shoes? Seems like the sensible choice to me. Of course, once the shoes were made and fitted, everything might have been reconsidered and running away could well have fallen down their list of priorities.

Mary Baker, sister to the infamously absconding Baker Boys, also appears in the stoppages ledger in 1830, a year after George was sent to prison and a full three years since Job ran away, never to return. On 12 June Mary also made a sizeable dent in the money owing to her. The hefty amount of 6s 6d appears against her name. She had bought a pair of new shoes . . .

The 'cash forfeited' tag was the fate of four girls between

1816 and 1821. Ann Tate was first in 1826, 'money forfeited'. Sarah England on 1 March 1817, 'money forfeited from account'. Mary Whitehead in 1819, and then Elizabeth Sullivan of Chelsea on 5 March 1821. Elizabeth forfeited £1 2s 3d, no mean sum. We can only assume that these girls did indeed abscond as there is no record of any cash being taken from those written down as runaways. Either the bookkeepers waited until there was no question of return, or the runaways left only debt. An unpaid debt would certainly explain the lengths the masters went to retrieve some of the runaways

Mary Coups was another single girl on the run and, for some considerable time, she must have thought she'd got away with it. Before her untimely disappearance, Mary had form. On 1 September 1821 she was fined 1s for breaking a window. On 1 March 1823 she was fined 2s for breaking two windows. Maybe she took the old adage 'pinch, punch, first of the month' too far? Mary elevated herself above the common crime of window-busting to disappear on 12 February 1824, and was not apprehended until August that same year. Almost six months on the run. Where did she manage to hide away so that the authorities could not find her? Did she flee further than the intrepid boys had done when running to London? Did she go even further to escape capture? Or did she hide in plain sight, under their noses? On 2 August 1824 Mary was returned by the not-so eagle-eyed constable of Wilmslow, from her hideaway some two miles down the road.

Catherine Quigley was another Liverpool lass with a turn of temper and seems to have been the only person ever to appear in the stoppages ledger for having a hissy fit. At least that's how it reads on first appraisal. In 1841 Catherine was fined 5s by Mr Fletcher, the mill manager, for 'standing on the lodge steps and going out'. It seems Catherine refused to cross the threshold and go back to work. This is the only record of such an act of open rebellion taking place. What on earth had happened to Catherine to make her opt for such a flagrant display of attitude? It was definitely understandable that apprentices would often not want to cross that threshold, but none seems to have disobeyed the manager like this. We need to go back four years to get to the heart of the matter, and like a lot of the tales, it begins with a running away. On 6 May 1837, the stoppages ledger reads that Catherine Quigley, of Liverpool, was fined a full 16s, having 'lost two weeks running away'. Intriguingly, there is no cost shown for her capture and return, as there was with the other Liverpool girls. Did she come back of her own volition? If so, why? We need to go even further back and to come up against remarkable similarities with the celebrated case of Esther Price.

In 1833 Mr and Mrs Shawcross, the Apprentice House superintendents, were summoned to give testimony before the Factory Commission, giving details of the lives of the apprentices and the care given at Quarry Bank. Part of their evidence stated that, 'children when they come first don't look so hearty as when they have been here some time, particularly when we get them from the Liverpool Workhouse'. If it really was the case that working in the mill actually improved your health and looks, then God help those who looked so sickly they were turned away. This evidence supports the theory that, back in the Liverpool Workhouse, assumptions were often made, with no baptismal certificates to hand, about a child's age, especially it seems when deeming them fit and old enough to be indentured. If they were too young they couldn't work, too old and their apprenticeship wouldn't last as long – they'd need to be either let go or be paid as an adult. Quite often, guesses were made, judged on size. Certainly Dr Holland at Quarry Bank often gives his opinion on the ages of newly arriving children when first examining them. So, a detailed analysis of Catherine Quigley's record should offer up more clues.

Initially it would have read that Catherine was indentured on 1 January 1834. Her age is given as eleven and she is to be apprenticed for eight years. Once at work in the mill, nothing is noted of Catherine until she runs away in 1837, almost a year after Esther Price had returned to Liverpool. Esther, making a stand with her sister Martha and John Doherty, was able to unearth her real baptismal record and prove her true age. She made the instant jump into adulthood and paid work. She secured her future. But Esther had to get herself locked up in solitary confinement with a dead person before she got her justice. Catherine's actions weren't so dramatic. She just stood in a doorway and refused to go any further. A further investigation of her indenture shows a later addition: 'Catherine Quigley left the Apprentice House on 24th April on producing the annexed certificate showing she was above twenty years of age.'

They had said she was eighteen years old when she was

over twenty. No wonder she refused to budge. This was no hissy fit, this was full-blown, justified anger at an awful wrong. And then, to cap it all, she was fined for the pleasure. Catherine appeared on the 1841 wages book, working in the first spinning room, but she doesn't seem to have the forgiveness or staying power of Esther. After this short spell in the spinning rooms, Catherine disappears from the records.

There were many reasons for the child apprentices to run away, all of them understandable. They had been duped into service, sold by the parishes, been orphaned or given up by struggling families. No child entered a mill with a smile on their face and they certainly never left there after a sixteen-hour shift grinning either. This system was the closest Britain had managed to get to the slave trade in Africa and the West Indies. Some children in the worst mills were treated almost as badly as those slaves, and few ever saw the mills as something they would have chosen for themselves. Once they were in, of course, everything changed. Then they were almost obliged to stay, shackled there either by debt or by duty to families. And this became a generational issue. Descendants of apprentices, those who were born into the system, literally had no choice. It was all their parents knew, and it soon became all they would know. Life after life, given up to the grinding, smashing, stretching and twisting of cotton. Except, of course, there was a choice. You could always run away. But being indentured meant that running away was a crime and in life, every crime, large or small, has its punishment.

CHAPTER SEVEN

Apples and Buckshot

So if, as a millowner in the eighteenth century, you decide against beating your child workers to within an inch of their lives as a punishment for any perceived crime, what else could you do? The Gregs seemed determined not to inflict physical pain on their charges; instead they chose to load them with debt after debt. A mountain of pennies on their young and slender shoulders. A real burden, and, in making every effort to relieve it, they just had to work all the harder. The greater the crime, the greater the fine.

Running away, of course, was the biggest misdemeanour but Esther, being Esther, made it into something even worse. On her recapture, she brought with her enough trouble to threaten the very fabric of the mill, and stretch the very limitations of what the Gregs were prepared to do to keep their workforce under the yoke.

Robert Hyde Greg, by now in charge at Quarry Bank, relates his version of what happened, via a transcript of a statement to the authorities regarding his treatment of Esther and Lucy. Interestingly, he begins by saying how the stewards of the Apprentice House changed in August 1835. The previous attendant, Mr Shawcross, had died some months earlier and Mrs Shawcross decided to leave after twenty-five years of service. Greg takes up the story: 'During his illness and subsequently, the children who had been in excellent order for 20 years became rather less tractable.' Biding their time like Esther, waiting for any chance, any chink in the armour of their masters? Perhaps it was simply the case that, once they detected a whiff of disorder, their previous adherence to whatever order had been maintained for those years started to melt away? In the same way that a class of children, in the absence of their regular teacher, will sorely test the mettle of the supply teacher in front of them for the day. Think you can rule over us? Think again.

Robert Hyde Greg lets the incoming stewards shoulder some of the blame: 'Mr and Mrs Timperley succeeded to the charge of the Apprentice House, for which they were perhaps not perfectly qualified.' Damned with faint praise? Whatever their failings, Esther didn't wait long before striking out. Robert Hyde explains: 'In November that same year, Esther Price and another girl committed so violent assault on a fellow apprentice that I sent them to the magistrates.' Notice that Esther gets the only name-check, although we strongly suspect that Lucy was her accomplice. Esther would have known of the possible consequences of her actions, so we can believe that she probably stored up all her grievances against the object of her anger and simply let loose. The Esther we see in the television series was a righter-of-wrongs with a strong sense of fairness. She stood up to bullies and protected her friends. Maybe this was an act of retribution, a wrong put right? After such a beating, who would stand against her? If she was prepared to face the magistrates in achieving what she thought was right, then nothing would stay her hand, and her enemies would have trembled at the prospect of crossing her. We do know that Esther harboured such a strong sense of justice that she later ran away to Liverpool to try and prove her real age, so this portrayal of her seems accurate. Clearly Robert Hyde Greg shared this sense of real justice in deciding that the magistrates were the natural course of action. We don't know what form he thought this justice would take, but it's safe to assume he didn't expect to hear the actual judgement passed down by the magistrates. Robert Hyde goes on: 'The Bench (Thomas Daintry and William Hope) declined committing and recommended that we should find some means at the home of checking disorders.'

So, at the very least, had Greg expected their committal? It must have been some beating. Being told, in so many words, to clean up his own backyard, would obviously give him a headache, especially with the Timperleys now in charge. Imagine, then, his annoyance, when finding that, on the very day of this decision, he had two more misbehaving girls to contend with. Sarah Crop and Isabella Shaw had just been recaptured after running away to Liverpool (where else?). Greg decided to act decisively. 'I ordered two disorderly girls a week of solitary confinement but released them on the fourth day.' Why on the fourth day? Was he softening already? In positions of great power, it is not always a good idea to backtrack on stern judgements, just because they are seen as stern, for fear of having this in itself perceived as a weakness. Perhaps Greg just wanted to show compassion, after what he deemed a stringent enough punishment? He certainly attempted to bolster this decision with a proviso: 'To deter any more from running away I announced to them publicly that I should resort to the old punishment of cutting off the hair of all future runaways.' This was what girls dreaded the most and I'm sure Greg said this with great solemnity and intent. Did he stick to it? Despite what we saw in the television series, emphatically no. The fictional Robert Hyde Greg forces Lucy to cut Esther's hair with what can only be described as a monstrous-looking pair of shears, the kind you might take to a sheep. It's a shocking moment and leaves the fictional Esther with a spiky crop of hair that she sports proudly for the rest of the series. In reality, this would have been the worst kind of punishment anyone could mete out to a girl; hence its dramatic power and use in the show. The prospect of a shorn head would have been a real deterrent, or so you would have thought.

It took less than a year for Esther and Lucy to decide to abscond to Liverpool. They did so at the end of Wakes' Week that year, August 1836, on a Saturday night. Greg recounts their eventual recapture: 'Lucy returned the Thursday following and Esther Price the Tuesday but one after. They said to some of their companions they did not care what was done with them, as long as their hair was not cut off.'

So Esther and Lucy had called Greg's bluff, and the

Apprentice House would have held its collective breath, awaiting the severity of the girls' fate. Greg's subsequent prevarication spoke volumes. 'On a consultation respecting the punishment, Mrs Shawcross and my sister Sally both remonstrated against the severity of cutting off girls' hair; and I requested my brother Sam to see the Magistrates, and know what punishment they would award if the girls were sent before them.'

Perhaps with the magistrates' previous words ringing in his ears, Greg does not wait for their disapproval. 'But the girls returning before an answer was obtained recollecting their charge and (concurring on the propriety) I ordered Lucy Garner three days' imprisonment and Esther Price a week's.' In an industry that occasionally suspended supposed miscreants over moving machinery for daring to work too slowly, this seems something of a cop-out. Perhaps, harshly, it could be said that the Gregs were too liberal for their own good? Or, more credibly, that they were human beings trying desperately hard to treat their employees with a modicum of decency as befitting a fellow human being and a person of lesser social standing? In this respect Robert Hyde was very much his mother's son. Perhaps a degree of mutual respect between him and Esther remained after the whole episode had drawn to a close? He had proved merciful and she had shown herself to be made of stern stuff. If indeed it did, the matter had not yet run its full course and Robert Hyde could never have guessed at its next development.

Lucy, on her return, was locked up in the Apprentice House. Greg notes this down for the authorities: 'Lucy Garner was confined in a spare bedroom all Friday, Saturday and Sunday, and I believe (for it seems uncertain) on Thursday night.' He goes on to tell of the conditions: 'She had porridge twice a day. The windows were not boarded up, and the weather being warm, and there being 60 or 80 woollen cloaks hanging up in the room, Mr Timperley did not think it necessary to put in a bed which he had for the girls confined the previous November.'

So far, so good. The lack of a bed seems a little harsh, but, then again, it was supposed to be a punishment. Also, it may seem strange that Robert Hyde is being so precise with his accounts. There are few other descriptions of what went on in the Apprentice House, unless they were being retold to the magistrates following some kind of official intervention. And what happened next certainly falls into that category. Robert Hyde must have been relieved to get Esther back and under lock and key. This dubious pleasure was not to last long. Greg continues: 'Esther Price came back after Lucy Garner was gone out and was confined in the same room. The windows were boarded, partly to prevent her escape and partly to prevent communication without. The room was partially dark.'

So, tougher measures for Esther. A maximum security set-up with no contact with the outside world. Fear of insurrection or just to put into Esther the fear of – if not God, then the next best thing, the Gregs? And, who knows, it may well have succeeded without a different kind of divine intervention. It wasn't Esther's meals that broke her resolve. 'Her food milk and porridge and bread, morning and evening same as the other girls, but no dinner.' She'd been hungry before, she could outlast this. Esther had been incarcerated from Monday to the Friday, but on that Friday, according to Greg, 'after all the girls were in bed, Mrs Timperley died of apoplexy'.

What were the chances? Robert Hyde must have felt cursed with bad luck, not to mention the poor Mrs Timperley. And what else to do with the body late on a Friday night, but to lay it to rest somewhere in the very house where the recently departed soul had lived, the Apprentice House? The choice of location could have been made more judiciously. In the dramatised series, Mrs Timperley was placed under a tarpaulin of sorts in the same room as Esther, and, having stood in that very room at the top of the house, my shoulders hunched against the sloping roof, I can attest as to the unsuitability of such a resting place. One body, yes. One body and a frightened young girl was never going to work out well. Greg's account tells it differently. 'On the following day, Esther Price feeling alarmed at being by herself, in the same house as the dead body begged to come out, promising to complete her term of imprisonment afterwards.' And, who, in all honesty, could blame her? There is no mention of how long she was left to plead for her release, just the following report: 'She was thereupon let out and never put in again.'

This, you might think, brought an unsavoury end to the whole episode. I'm certain Robert Hyde would have wished that it had. Far from it. In many ways the death of Mrs Timperley (who gets forgotten in the following rumpus) is just the start of a bigger, longer-lasting story, resulting in the elevation of Esther to the ranks of causes célèbres and making her into the poster girl for female apprentices.

On her release from the room, Lucy wrote to her mother back in Liverpool, presumably complaining about her unjust treatment, and apparently claiming that she and Esther had simply 'extended' their Wakes' Week holiday by a couple of days and weren't absconding at all. In no time at all Robert Hyde was entertaining the joint forces of a parish commissioner from Liverpool, Mr Turner of the Short Time Committee, and a certain John Doherty, famed pamphleteer and stirrer of wasps' nests. Robert Hyde Greg finds himself and his factory under great scrutiny, hence his carefully worded report to the magistrates. The girls, however, begged to differ, and told an ever-so-slightly different story. Whatever grudging respect may have been building between Esther and Robert Hyde was about to be sorely tested.

The resulting fallout from that first visit exists in the form of another visit, this time on 8 January 1837, and this time in the shape of John Doherty and a Mrs Doughty, otherwise known as Martha, Esther's older sister. The two are reputed to have met in the nearby Horseshoe Inn and it is thought that Martha had brought along a very important document – Esther's baptismal certificate. This document was later discovered as being attached to her indenture, with the following written by hand at the top: 'Esther claims she will be 18 in March 1838.' So, presumably in a fury over her treatment at the hands of Robert Hyde, and determined to be out of the Apprentice House as soon as possible, Esther was willing to take them all on – again. Martha and Doherty were supposedly getting together to present a deposition, potentially taking Esther's case to court. This deposition would have told Esther's side of the story, her flight and subsequent imprisonment, but strangely it did not survive as a document. Was Esther's version squashed in an attempt to cloud the issue with half truths and rumours, leaving only Robert Hyde's version as the sole telling of the tale? It didn't work. In 1838 an anonymous pamphleteer published an essay entitled 'Misrepresentations exposed in a letter to Lord Ashley containing strictures of the Factory Acts as it affects the cotton manufacturer'. Not the catchiest of titles, but with an incendiary content. The essay attacked Robert Hyde Greg, citing his own previously published essay entitled 'The Factory Question', which argued against the Ten Hour Movement, whose aim was to reduce the working days of child workers in the cotton mills. Before we consider the content, we should consider the anonymity of the author. The detail therein could only have been written by someone with insider knowledge and access to Esther and Lucy. Maybe a clue could be found in the name of the publisher of the pamphlet? John Doherty. Not so much a single thorn in the side of cotton manufacturers and the Gregs in particular, but more of a thicket. The pamphlet tells a different story to Robert Hyde's.

The anonymous author tells us that Esther did not run away as such, she merely stretched out her Wakes' holiday a tad. Having asked for permission to visit her father during a 'temporary stoppage' of the works, she'd had this request denied. So, being Esther, she went anyway. The mill was to stop working during the Monday and Tuesday, all Esther did was to leave on the Saturday, Sunday being a day of rest anyway, and return on the Wednesday. She then allegedly worked until breakfast on that day before being whisked off to solitary confinement. Then, after suffering the horror of imprisonment with the Timperley corpse and, after her pleading had presumably fallen on deaf ears, instead of being humanely released, she'd been obliged to flee, having 'rushed past the person' bringing her midday meal the day after the death. Esther claimed that she 'would not remain whatever the consequences'. So, in the television dramatisation we have an amalgam of the truth with a peppering of both versions, sometimes the best way to tell a story.

Robert Hyde refuted this version, complaining that the authors had colluded and, 'told [him] the story with every kind of gross exaggeration and falsehood'. Greg went on to consult his attorneys to see if the Short Time Committee 'could not be prosecuted for a libel and conspiracy'. The gloves, had they ever been completely on, were now well and truly off. How Robert Hyde must have rued his softly-softly approach to Esther and Lucy! Why didn't he just sack them? He'd done it for lesser crimes than theirs. It seemed a race had begun between Esther and Robert Hyde. Prove your age and leave, indenture complete, or be dismissed for any number of transgressions. Surely there was now no going back for both these proud and determined individuals? Amazingly, there was.

A close reading of the documentation of the time shows

some seemingly minor discrepancies between Robert Hyde's account and the entries in the stoppages ledger. Robert Hyde states that Esther returned on the Tuesday, the ledger has Monday. Esther's absence is handwritten in the ledger, Lucy's is not. Robert Hyde recalls they went at the end of Wakes' Week and the pamphlet mentions a mill holiday. In 1835 Esther had actually been allowed some time in Liverpool with her mother – it's entered in the ledger of the time. So, an allowed absence was not without precedent, and Esther did claim she'd asked for some leave, although denied. Did these muddied waters allow for a thaw in the frozen attitudes of Esther and Robert Hyde? If they did, strangely the thaw did not extend to best mate Lucy. The stoppages ledger actually shows that Esther did not even have to work overtime to make up for her absence. Then, with the benefit of hindsight, Robert Hyde writes an addendum to his account of the affair in 1843: 'This written immediately after the circumstances took place thinking it possible some statements might be made at some future time when no opportunity would exist of contradicting.' So, perhaps a deal was done between Esther and Robert Hyde. Despite her grievances against her employers, Esther never speaks in a derogatory manner about them, and she had plenty of opportunities.

John Doherty had had the Gregs in his sights for some time; he must surely have exerted some pressure on Esther to add her voice to the clamour of the Dissenters desperate to bring about change in the cotton industry. In the television series Esther does this, manning the barricades and leading the fight. In reality she fades from public view after asserting her true age and freeing herself from her indenture. All Robert Hyde would have had to say was along the lines of, if you want to remain employed here, we must have no more dissension. Whereas previously Esther might have told him where to stick his spinning machines, this new Esther is looking forward to a new life, as we shall see in the next chapter, and she rolled over. A deal obviously suited them both and probably infuriated John Doherty, who was offered few cast-iron chances to get under the collective skins of the Greg family. Esther and most of her batch of apprentices were kept on after attaining eighteen years of age and finishing their indentures. Lucy was not.

While the major dramas of running away and retribution were being played out, there were a whole lot of other offences waiting to be committed by angry, frustrated child apprentices. As we have seen, the Gregs did not allow physical punishment for their workers, though what went on under their paternalistic radar is a matter of conjecture. Because it wasn't official, it doesn't mean that it never happened. Exasperated overlookers, under pressure themselves, would maybe clout a child round the ear for being slow, or cheeky. But certainly there was nothing remotely like the level of abuse suffered at Litton Mill. In Quarry Bank, debt was a greater motivator than pain. When a misdemeanour merited a fine, the sum was subtracted from the offender's meagre savings. If the fine was greater than the savings, then the offender went into the Gregs' debt and had to work for nothing to pay it all back, to the penny. Depending on the amount owed, this could take months, especially for apprentices whose only earnings came from overtime, at a penny per hour.

Leafing through the stoppages ledger, where all crime is laid bare to see, we can glean that the lads at the mill were fixated on stealing apples and breaking windows. Hardly the acts of master criminals, but for the perpetrators they were wilful acts of rebellion, a smack in the eye for authority. A way of kicking back against the endless grind, fear and sheer boredom of mill life. It was a way of establishing your identity, regaining some small sliver of that humanity surrendered to the toil.

One particular escapade was described in Thomas Tonge's 'Recollections'. It involves a late-night sortie that didn't work out well. James Sparks was an apprentice who worked in the 'blowing' rooms, carding and scutching, that is. He would have savoured any freedom from those infernal places that he could get, and he certainly savoured any delicacies he could get his hands on. Given the unimaginative food doled out to the apprentices, it was no surprise that sweet things, such as apples, were considered a delicacy. Apprentices would go to great lengths to obtain these prizes. The resulting penalties, if caught, were financially tough. A fine for stealing apples was 5s, a lot of overtime at a penny an hour, and 'Old Shawcross', the Apprentice House steward at the time, was a known disciplinarian. So when James, aided and abetted by some mates from the Apprentice House, used the cover of darkness to steal away from the house, they knew the possible and dire consequences.

We can only assume there was some light from the moon, as they first had to climb out of the windows. If they were sleeping in the upper floors of the house, then this escape is all the more daring. Rather than set off over to the Greg gardens, or indeed the family's own orchards, James and his gang set off for the trees they knew to be heavy with apples in the grounds of one Thomas Dale of Morley. What an adventure, creeping silently through the Apprentice House gardens, over the gate and scampering away down the lane towards Morley, glancing over their shoulders to make sure no light appeared in the house's black, blind windows. How they must have celebrated their ingenuity, and how they must have slavered with anticipation at the thought of the apples waiting for them.

The apples weren't the only thing waiting in the orchard, however. The lads hadn't factored Thomas Dale himself into their plans, or if they had, surely he wouldn't be skulking around his orchards at night for no good reason? And, all right, if he was, what's the worst he could do to them, at his age? Chase them? Not a chance, they were too fleet of foot. At worst they'd catch an unlucky glance from a lucky swing on Thomas's part with whatever stick he could find to hand. And there was no way on earth he could identify them, not at night. Besides, they were comparatively many to his few. Even if one copped for it, the others would make good their escape, laden with apples. If any of the lads had thought more deeply about a worst-case scenario they might have considered that Thomas would not only be up and about, but that he'd be very much alert and holding his gun. And that the gun would be loaded.

So, when picking their way gingerly through the trees, imagine their surprise to be confronted by what no one had foreseen. Thomas Dale probably shouted a warning as he levelled his gun at them. The lads may have scorned him, they may even have continued stealing the apples. Whatever they did, it was enough to precipitate Thomas's next action. Firing 'what he thought was a gun simply loaded with powder, to frighten the lads' he must have been horrified to see lead pellets peppering the figures fleeing before him. Seemingly James had been the unluckiest, the most foolhardy or the bravest, for he was the lad closest to Thomas, who had 'planted a dozen pellets into Sparks which, while increasing his running powers for the next half mile, prevented, for days, his sitting down with comfort'. All bravado gone in the blast of a gun. A searing pain in his arse and a breathless sprint out of Morley, apples a distant memory.

Back in the Apprentice House, James's next problem, a pressing one, was to avoid the detection of Old Shawcross. The buckshot had to come out and his mates had the answer. There was nothing they could do about the pellet holes in his pants, but his backside was another matter – 'his companions did their best to pick out the shot with the point of a pocket knife blade'. That must have made for a sorry sight should they have awoken any of their fellow bed mates on their return. It's hard to believe there was even an ounce of dignity left for James, arse in the air and a rag clenched between his teeth in case he cried out as his mates dug away at his burning, reddened skin. There is no record of any repercussions from this episode, and James was probably perversely grateful to have been on his feet the whole of the next day. We can only assume they got away with it, if being shot in the backside and tearing home apple-less is getting away with it.

In terms of fines, stealing – when detected – was up there with the worst. Theft, it seemed, would not be tolerated. Breaking windows also seemed to occur in almost epidemic proportions and, quite often, on a Friday. One theory goes that with Friday being pay-day, smashing a window was like putting two fingers up to the masters. It was possibly even done under the influence of whatever alcoholic mixture the culprit got their hands on. It's Friday night, they had pennies in their pockets . . . money to burn, why not show your anger, your frustration? If you were caught you were fined the princely sum of around a shilling or more, and wasn't that worth it when you saw your stone whistle over the river and find its target, that sweet sound of cracking glass echoing across the darkening meadow? To many of the lads it certainly was.

Lads like William Owen, who was indentured to Quarry Bank on 8 March 1819, aged nine years. His indenture is signed by the overseers of the poor for Altrincham and reads that it is to run for seven years. William appears in Dr Holland's treatment list twice, but only for an emetic and white powder. His initial examination has him down as healthy. He certainly had nothing wrong with his throwing arm. Maybe for his first two years at the mill, he went out and practised in the meadow, picking out trees, or places in the riverbank? Maybe he was putting in the overtime, saving every hard-earned penny. Then on 3 March 1821, only five days short of his second anniversary there, William has a bit of a blow-out. The stoppages ledger spells out his spree: 'To three lamp glasses 4s 6d. To two square windows 2s.' Six shillings and sixpence.

Did they stop him as he was preparing to throw yet another stone? Maybe William had counted up his savings and thought he'd stop just short of going into debt? Or maybe he just lost it and raged against his fate? It took him two years before he was caught again, as there is no evidence tying him in with any other broken windows in the meantime. The ledger for 1 March 1823 reads: 'To two broken windows 2s.' March again, anniversary time. Then again, a year later on 1 March, 'To one window 1s.' Either William was slowing down, or maybe just getting better, honing his skill and taking just the one shot to break the one window. Thus satisfied, he stood, arms folded, awaiting his capture? The following year there are no entries for William, so either he didn't mark his anniversary or he wasn't caught. Perhaps he was simply marking his time at Quarry Bank. The following year, on 11 March, there is a final entry in the memoranda, 'Out of his time.' William was gone, and his future? He joined the army, presumably as a crackshot.

James Morrall could be said to be the king of broken windows. Not for the sheer number he shattered, but for the quality. On 20 May 1816 he was charged a full eight shillings for breaking a window in the Gregs' house. Given that it was unlikely he could have got close enough to despatch a window at the front of the house, overlooking the gardens and river, we can only assume it was thrown as he passed the entrance of the house, the one closest to the apprentice way into the mill. Venting your frustration with your hated and feared place of work was one thing, but taking it out on the very house of your master called for a different kind of resentment. Perhaps James wanted to strike at the Greg children who probably slept in these upstairs rooms? It was an expensive form of protest. James went on to break only one more window, an ordinary 2s 8d one, in 1819. In 1825 he is registered as being 'Out of his time without permission'. He'd gone, on the day his indenture came to an end, without a by-your-leave.

Thinking of those boys, bound as they were to a system through no fault of their own, and with no discernible end in sight, who can begrudge the odd stone thrown in anger and bitter frustration? It's a wonder there was any glass left intact at all.

We shouldn't leave girls out of the picture. They were just as capable as boys when it came to smashing windows, as a close inspection of the stoppages ledger reveals. Not least Hannah Morrall, sister of James, evidently keeping it in the family. No doubt small acts of wanton rebellion were as satisfying an outlet for girls as they were for boys. And of course, on a more serious level, were the strikingly similar acts of rebellion by Esther Price and Catherine 'hissy fit' Quigley.

Of course, there is one misdemeanour that only girls could

commit, not so much a rebellion as a basic fact of life, and for this act they certainly needed a partner-in-crime. They could get pregnant, strictly against the terms of their indenture (though they probably weren't thinking about that at the time). Not that this was a frequently recorded occurrence. Maria Hough suffered the painful ignominy of being the only girl ever let go for such a 'crime'. She appears in the stoppages ledger between 1818 and 1825 for less grievous sins, including, unsurprisingly, smashing a window. The last record of her reads 'discharged being pregnant'. After this, she disappears, with no existing medical notes. A harsh punishment for a young girl probably too scared to do anything about her pregnancy until it was too late and she was cast adrift into a perilous world with a bastard baby imminent.

Contrast this with the treatment meted out to Susanna Catterall. She provides us with the only case of an apprentice girl where a pregnancy is registered as having gone full term. Far from dismissing her out of hand for breach of contract, the Gregs paid for her confinement. Such a gesture obviously fuelled many conspiracy theories about Susanna and the mystery father of her child, one of which was dealt with in the television series as a liaison between Susanna and William Greg. Here, the engineer Daniel Bate is her saviour, asking her to marry him (though in real life he would have had to have been working at the mill for over half a century by this time). It certainly wasn't William, so the question still hangs there: why did the Gregs pay for this child to be born? Could it have been that Susanna kept the pregnancy secret for too long for any kind of abortion to be carried out, and, if so, then why did this not apply to the unfortunate Maria Hough? Was she too good a worker to simply let go? Was the father someone of standing in the mill, already married, with a secret to be kept? Was it simply altruism, born out of a real affection for Susanna? Whatever the reason, this was still a business and the costs always had to be recouped. Susanna had to pay back the full amount of the confinement on her return to work. If the child was the result of an illicit relationship with any Greg male, do we believe that they would run the risk of putting Susanna back in the mill to pay off her debts?

This bill survives in the archives, having been sent by one Isaac Shawcross, dated 7 June 1842. (It could well be that Isaac was a relative of the late George Shawcross, a former Apprentice House superintendent.) There is the following account:

To 9 weeks Board and Lodging (Susanna Catterall)	£2.5.0.
To attendance during confinement	5.0.
To midwife	2.6.
	£2.2.6

Debts must be repaid.

Apples and buckshot, the crime and the punishment. Was this a fair and even-handed system? When Robert Hyde Greg actually sought out the due process of law with Esther and Lucy, the magistrates batted it back to him. Sort out your own messes any way you deem appropriate. If you overstep the mark, we'll upbraid you publicly. The Gregs were determined not to beat their apprentices and so punished them financially, binding them further and for longer and getting more work out of them in the process. Would some have preferred to have got a beating out of the way and carried on, suitably chastised, their time their own? In the darker, more satanic mills of Manchester, they'd have received a thousand times worse, some beaten so badly they feared for their lives. Of course, it should be sufficient to say that these unfortunate children should never have been in this position in the first place, but that's easy to say from the safety of twenty-first-century Britain.

Perhaps the saddest case of a punishment not fitting the crime recorded in the mill's archives was in the fate of William Potts. This time it wasn't stealing apples or smashing windows that got William into trouble. It was taking a risk, a high-spirited risk, in his own time. The Gregs knew better than most that boys will be boys and, who knows, had they witnessed what William did on that day, they might not even have upbraided him for it. The introduction of weaving to Quarry Bank would claim its first fatality and not a shuttle in sight.

The huge new weaving looms had been dragged from the meadows into the mill on planks laid over the Bollin, a few feet above the river's racing currents. As if this wasn't dangerous enough, recent rains had swollen the Bollin to flood levels and it surged beneath the bouncing, mossy planking. By

12 February 1835 a single plank remained in place. On their lunch break that day, a group of mill lads gathered around it on the meadow side, daring each other to cross it. William Potts took up the challenge. Egged on by the others, he set off across the plank. Hovering above the muddy Bollin he would have felt the rush of cold air coming off the roaring river, he'd have had the crash of the water surging over the weir in his ears along with the joshing of his mates. This being February he probably still wore his clogs, their hard wooden soles offering little purchase on the slippery plank. Did he ever stop to contemplate what would happen if he slipped? Perhaps he believed the river held no real threat – he'd possibly swam and maybe even bathed in it from time to time. But not at full spate, not like this day, not in February. The Bollin was never clear at the best of times, washing down, as it did, the effluence from other mills further up stream. But when in flood, it would have carried branches and trailed weeds like snags, snatching careless animals from its banks, drowning them and offering their bloated bodies up downstream as carrion for the crows. In the blink of an eye William would have been off the plank and under the freezing water, the cold and speed of the rush taking his breath away. He may not even have had time to kick off his useless clogs as the towering walls of the mill flashed by him. He would have sought in vain to feel the river bed beneath his outstretched feet and his arms would have flailed, equally in vain, to keep his head above water. His mates would have had to sprint along the grassy banks of the river to keep up. In seconds he would have passed under the bridge

separating the Greg house from the mill, maybe watched by disbelieving workers from the mill windows. Did he shout out, attracting the attention of anyone in the Greg gardens? The gardeners, the Greg children, the masters themselves? The only record of the awful event tells us that, 'notwithstanding every effort made to rescue him he was carried down the stream and drowned'.

The river was 'frequently dragged for a considerable distance', presumably by volunteers from the mill and the village. Maybe even by William's own family. They would have searched with dread, as the victims of drowning do not improve their appearance with age and exposure to the water. Maybe some even secretly prayed that they did not find him, so they could remember him as he'd been, a lively and certainly mischievous boy. As with most river deaths, the most likely cause of his drowning was being clutched at from beneath, snagged by his clothing and held underwater long enough to force that last breath from his lungs. Then he'd have swayed with the current like all the other dead things. Until that is the river was ready to give him up. Records show that six or seven weeks passed before the River Bollin flooded again. This time, whatever grabbed and held William was itself overwhelmed and the currents dragged him free. His body appeared thus: 'It rose to the surface at the next flood being found between Northcliffe and Oversley Ford.' Up to seven weeks in a river flush with rats and fish would not have been kind to poor William, and some compassion needs to be spared for those who found him. The mill documents his death with the following words: '1 killed by accident but at play not in the mill.'

William paid the ultimate price for his seemingly small act of rebellion, not to the Gregs but to fate, resulting in his death. For Susanna and Maria, the price of their foray into the realms of criminality was that they created a life. In the way that William surely did not begin that precarious walk with the expectation of dying, the girls probably did not succumb to their amorous encounter with the sure knowledge that they'd become pregnant. They all took chances, it was part of what helped them feel more alive. For the girls, a lifetime's responsibility followed a few snatched moments of pleasure, but isn't that often the case when the chance you take involves plunging into the murky waters of love and sex?

CHAPTER EIGHT

LOVE AND SEX

The onset of sexuality must have hit some of our apprentices like an onrushing train. Little prepared, they'd have stood blinking in its path, arms wide for whatever it held and promised, or curled, ball-like, threatened and terrified by the very same things. Yet, like all trains, they'd have heard it coming from some distance. All those raging hormones, crammed under the one roof of the Apprentice House. No sex education, apart from the ill-advised rumours whispered from one apprentice to another in the bible-black nights of the dorms and flushed from their febrile imaginations. For the boys, the tantalising proximity of the girls, their particular smell, the promise of something forbidden. For the girls, that strange mix of fear and thrill based on rumour and storytelling. Every part of human nature not ground down by brutal work would have been stored and treasured until those delicious moments of comparative freedom on Sunday afternoons, or Wakes' days when, unshackled from the mill, they could give full vent to their sexual and emotional longings. A sexual dance of expectation, trepidation and unfulfilled longing.

With sexual ignorance and such a large, mixed, workforce, it's surprising that more babies weren't born to girl apprentices. There are just the records of poor Maria Hough, discharged in disgrace, and Susanna Catterall, mysteriously allowed to come to term before she worked off her debt and disappeared. Maybe one reason was delayed maturity: most mill girls, malnourished, overworked and underdeveloped, possibly did not hit puberty until perhaps as old as fifteen or sixteen. There are no instances of treatment for menstrual pain in these records, unless they are alluded to in the dealings with stomach pains. Once a girl was menstruating and sexually active, she was of course at risk of pregnancy. For all her ignorance, she'd know that. At the very least she'd have been given a 'rag' by the Apprentice House stewardess at the first signs, even if it meant chucking out the soiled straw from their cot in the morning.

A common explanation is offered by the fiction of Hedley Smith (1909–92), who in his novella *The Mill Folk*, about working people in a northern cotton mill, gives us a female character called Martha Danby, who quotes the following passage to her niece for advice on sexual matters:

> 'Of course I had my fun with the lads in my time. But I were smart enough to know when to keep the gate shut . . . And it's been a lot happier and more sensible life than tewing your guts out at a loom all day, and then coming home to breed babbies all night to follow on in your footsteps at the mill.'

This passage, although fictional, rings absolutely true. The only failsafe method of protection against pregnancy was abstinence, at some point of the sexual encounter, and keeping 'the gate shut' was as good a way as any. Clearly, there were times when keeping the gate shut was either abandoned or simply not shut quickly enough. Statistics at the time reveal that around 40 per cent of women married for the first time were already pregnant. But if marriage wasn't an option, what was a girl to do?

One clue might lie in the contents of the Apprentice House garden – and you won't find it in the exhaustive list of remedies left by the imperious Dr Holland. I asked chemist and current volunteer Philip Charnley what a girl would do if she found herself pregnant with what was almost always an unwanted baby. He didn't hesitate: pennyroyal. To get a full and detailed description of this herb and its properties, I consulted the marvellous *Culpeper's Complete Herbal* by the seventeenth-century botanist, astrologer and physician Nicholas Culpeper. Pennyroyal (*Mentha pulegium*) has remarkable properties: 'This herb is under Venus. It makes thin, tough phlegm, warms any part to which it is applied and digests corrupt matter.' Then to the matter in hand: 'If boiled and drank, it provokes women's courses and expels the dead child and afterbirth.' Philip remembers people asking for this 'pennyroyal and steel' over his father's chemist counter as late as the 1950s.

Culpeper adds other parts of the body to the list of pennyroyal's applications. The stomach, eyes, joints, toothache, pains of breast or belly, ulcers, cramps or convulsions, all to be treated by the same herb. Walking through the garden today, it's easy to overlook this small, innocuous plant. It's low to the ground and looks like cress. Plucking and rubbing the green leaves between your fingers releases a slightly peppery, minty aroma. It's a welcoming, palliative smell, promising calm. Everything about pennyroyal belies its powerful properties, a handful being capable of provoking such an extreme result.

Few of the apprentice girls themselves would have known about the application of pennyroyal and its terrible properties. Any terrified and clueless girl would have sought the advice of a hopefully understanding adult, or they would have paid for it. A village such as Wilmslow would have a herbalist, and after a lengthy walk and the handing over of a shilling or two, the deed would have been done, and no one the wiser – with the obvious exception of the pregnant girl herself, left to trudge back to Styal on her own, the griping cramps beginning to take hold and faced with the awful knowledge of what was about to happen to her. As the stewards of the Apprentice House were in charge of the gardens, they must have known of its use and probably engaged in its preparation and dispensing. The abortion of the foetus and the expelling of the afterbirth and any amount of bleeding would also have been difficult to hide, even if it was only noticed when the laundry was done.

Were the apprentice girls any different from teenage girls today who find themselves needing a morning-after pill following a hasty, ill-advised, regretted or forced assignation? The apprentice girls certainly wouldn't have wanted any pregnancy to come to the attention of the millowners and managers. After all, the Health and Morals of Apprentices Act of 1802 stipulated that the sexes should be segregated, and no millowner wanted to attract undue attention from the authorities, especially where illicit pregnancy was concerned. As if a simple Act of Parliament was ever going to stop any lovesick boy or girl, once their blood was up . . .

But if pennyroyal didn't work, what then? Attempt to hide your unruly and swollen belly as it defied your every wish and grew and grew? At least one girl managed this feat. Records in Styal village tell of a baby being abandoned on a doorstep in the village. The mother was never found, and the baby was whisked off to Wilmslow police station. If the mother was a mill girl, it couldn't have been easy to keep such a secret in the hothouse atmosphere of the Apprentice House and the work rooms. Imagine feeling that child growing inside you and knowing that you had left it too late to abort the foetus and that the very thing you were carrying would bring about your downfall? Maybe the young mother-to-be had tried pennyroyal and just got sick for her troubles, or perhaps she genuinely hadn't realised until that very first stab of a contraction took her breath away. Sadly, the location of the doorstep and the identity of the householder are not recorded, so it is only possible to conjecture whether or not there was any significance in the desperate mother's choice when it came to laying the swathed baby down on the cold stone steps outside the door. She must have given birth alone, shocked and frightened at what was happening to her, and most probably just outside the village. It would have been impossible to deliver the baby inside the Apprentice House, or in the vicinity of the mill, where workers thronged. As babies are never masters or mistresses of their own timing, the mother must have been extremely lucky to have gone into labour at a convenient hour, and certainly not on the Gregs' time, although I sincerely doubt that the poor girl ever saw that luck played any part of what happened to her.

In order to gain a fuller picture of what it must have been like for young men and girls throughout the period of theapprenticeship system, we must take into consideration the sexual mores of the period: from the late eighteenth century to the middle of the nineteenth. To take a broad-brush view, the Georgians, popularly remembered for licentiousness under the dissolute George IV, had their sexual liberties washed away by a tide of Evangelical Christianity, making way for the full-blown Victorian ideal of denial and abstinence. After the war with Napoleon and under the growing influence of the middle classes, and indeed, merchants like the Gregs, Britain became a more serious place, at least in public. It is said that by the 1830s Lord Palmerston was the only remaining politician still wearing rouge in Parliament. Suddenly sex was off the agenda – or if it was on it, it had to be controlled. Of course we can never know the intimacy of lives that stayed behind closed doors; there has to be a lot of inference and implication. But the official line was clear: chastity and fidelity were the ideals. And masturbation was the new evil. It was a sin, and was actually dangerous to health (symptoms probably including blindness and hairy hands); it most certainly led to insanity. Men were now being counselled to conserve vital health by avoiding fornication outside marriage, and, to help curb 'nocturnal emissions', by rationing sex within marriage. And no masturbation, ever.

The girls were not to get off lightly either, as ailments and afflictions suffered by adolescent girls was said to signify 'abnormal sexual excitation'. Some doctors in certain circles actually used clitoridectomies to prevent sexual pleasure, one Dr Isaac Brown advocating that this horrendous procedure be recommended to eradicate the act of female self-abuse. These days, of course, this is recognised as mutilation. So people born into this age were to be factually uninformed and become sexually and emotionally frigid. Sexual strictures were defined by the upper classes, the religious and political establishment, endorsed by the middle class, and were impressed upon, rather than being wholeheartedly embraced by, the working classes. Indeed, some of the working class took no notice at all. In his 1844 classic *The Condition of the Working Class in England*, Engels observed social and sexual mores in Manchester:

> The husband works the whole day through, perhaps the wife and also the elder children, all in different places; they meet night and morning only, all under perpetual temptation to drink; what family life is possible under such conditions? Yet the working-man cannot escape from the family, must live in the family, and the consequence is a perpetual succession of family troubles, domestic quarrels, most demoralising for parents and

> children alike. Neglect of all domestic duties, neglect of the children, especially, is only too common among the English working people . . .

The men seem to come off worse: 'Next to intemperance in the enjoyment of intoxicating liquors, one of the principal faults of English working-men is sexual licence.'

Of course there's a world of difference between the squalor of Manchester slums, with alehouses and whorehouses, and the remote wooded womb of Quarry Bank. Here there was just the Ship Inn in Styal, and certainly no whorehouses. Not much opportunity for unbridled drinking and sexual excess, although according to Tonge, many did their level best.

In the first series of the television series we hear a male overlooker described in flat, neutral tones as a 'beard-splitter', a shockingly graphic term for a man with voracious sexual appetites and many 'conquests', mostly presumably non-consensual. We sense a dulled acceptance of the way things are deemed to unfold. Men do what they do, women accommodate them, especially if the man is in a position of power. Although there is no written evidence of abuse recorded at Quarry Bank, other mills have given up some of their terrible secrets. And the rot starts at the top. Engels describes factory owners thus:

> It is, besides, a matter of course that factory servitude, like any other, and to an even higher degree, confers the *jus primae noctis* upon the master. In this respect also the employer is sovereign over the persons and charms

> of his employees. The threat of discharge suffices to overcome all resistance in nine cases out of ten, if not in ninety-nine out of a hundred, in girls who, in any case, have no strong indictments to chastity. If the master is mean enough . . . his mill is also his harem; and the fact that not all manufacturers use their power, does not in the least change the position of the girls. In the beginning of manufacturing industry, when most of the employers were upstarts without education or consideration for the hypocrisy of society, they let nothing interfere with the exercise of their vested rights.

Engels visited Quarry Bank in 1845, and came away with an impression that did little to confirm his beliefs. He wrote of being confronted by guarded officials and smiling 'compliant' workers, those evidently in a state of 'beguiled slavery'. It is nigh on impossible to believe that any child would be treated in this way at Quarry Bank, and certainly no Greg would have countenanced it, but we can only guess at what happened in the shadowy recesses of the mill building. Simply because it wasn't reported doesn't mean it didn't happen. If we look at industrialisation in Yorkshire over the same period, we can see just how millhands and children were treated, sexually. There was violent sexual antagonism between the growing female factory workforce in Bradford, Yorkshire, and the *Yorkshire Factory Times* reported that 'attacks by men on women operatives' were alleged to be common occurrences. There are tales of how young male factory workers were in the habit of ritually humiliating female workers by shouting 'naughty and pert obscenities' when lasses in the cotton mills removed their stockings before work. There is also reported evidence of these same lads pulling up the clothes of female sleepers during their rest periods. In the late nineteenth century, as people began to feel that they had more of a voice to publicly air their grievances, letters to the newspaper reported an incident of an overseer disciplining one young female spinner by 'throwing up her skirts and smacking her with his hand', which her family viewed as a sexual assault.

There is also an explanation as to how any worker, especially female, could curry favour with their male overlookers, in order to increase or maintain their workload when they actually received payment for doing so. Another letter to the newspaper, from a woman weaver, described the 'tickling' of an overseer in a dark corner of the weaving shed. And so it was stated that sometimes, to keep your hand in at work, you had to keep your hand in your boss's trousers. Without the comparative freedom felt by these later millworkers to speak out loud, we would never be able to contemplate what happened in less enlightened times. The apprentices at Quarry Bank were human beings, like all their counterparts in the other cotton mills, and, like them, would have fallen prey to human nature in all its manifold forms of behaviour.

We can contrast sharply the choices available to the millworkers as opposed to their masters, the Gregs, when it came to matters of the heart. From the frenzied coupling that must have taken place among the apprentices, in the privies, in the woods, in any secluded place that allowed a degree of secrecy for these snatched moments of desire and folly, to the stately procession of the chaperoned courting of the Greg family.

A letter in 1817 from Robert Hyde Greg to his brother Samuel Jnr praises Grace Fletcher of Edinburgh, someone he met 'on tour' in Spain. He calls her a 'bluestocking', and tells Samuel, 'but though she possesses very extensive information, I don't think she in the least makes a parade of it, and when that is the case, learning in a woman is tolerable.'

Far from being the bumptious ramblings of a dyed-in-the-wool chauvinist, this was part of the prevailing attitude towards women in the nineteenth century. Robert Hyde goes on to venture that Grace would make a good wife for Samuel. It was often the fervent hope of parents that by parading their daughters on tour in Europe, they would indeed snag an eligible man of wealth and status and make a good marriage. In 1818 Robert Hyde meets the family again but Grace has died. Shaking off what he must have felt about this tragedy, he remains undecided which remaining daughter to choose. 'My heart remains my own, as it did in Spain, merely from my not being able to determine on which to bestow it. If you would take one you could greatly relieve me from my difficulty.'

The bestowing of one's heart must have been an onerous task, so much so that he tries to enlist his younger brother's aid in whittling down the candidates. We cannot imagine that such a wealth of choice stretched in front of our apprentices.

Esther Price, as she does in the second television series, takes up with William Whittaker, native of Styal and son of Abraham and Esther. He was a shoemaker, a simple man with an honest trade. She was an ex-apprentice who had fought the system, fought the Gregs, fought the law and fought with her fellow apprentices. William stood no chance. I searched in vain for any record of Esther having bought some shoes off William, as shown in flirtatious detail in the television series. It's a lovely thought and entirely in keeping with what we have gleaned about Esther's character – and she must have got shoes from somewhere . . . Having battled to record her true age, Esther wasted no time asserting her rights. After the controversy surrounding her act of absconding and John Doherty's intervention, her date of birth was confirmed as 8 March 1820. So in March 1838 Esther quits the Apprentice House. By May of 1839 she is giving birth to her and William's first child, also named William. Perhaps more remarkable than William Whittaker's swift capitulation is the fact that the Gregs allowed Esther to stay on after all the trouble she had caused them. Baby William's birth certificate names William Whittaker as the father, and, next to her name, Esther has placed a cross. Whether this first child was born after an intense period of courting once Esther had lodgings of her own, and therefore the privacy, isn't known. She and William wait another three years before she gives birth to their second child: Thomas Price was baptised at Norcliffe Chapel, Styal, in September 1843, also illegitimate.

Sometimes it takes just a few simple figures to hint at a greater story, stark figures masking a world of pain. Esther's name appears in the mill wages books for the first time in April

1840, where she is listed as working in the third spinning room. For this she was being paid 7s a week. Then we see her transferred to the reeling room, where she earned 8s a week. There is one period when her earnings drop. In the week commencing 5 November 1840, Esther's wages dropped to 2s 8d. This was the week of baby William's death, aged eighteen months. Esther lost 5s 4d – and her first-born son, still illegitimate.

So, why didn't Esther and William marry as soon as she became pregnant, as was the custom of the time? Why perservere, apart, still having children, and not make things easier for themselves? For me, the answer lies with William's parents, Abraham and Esther. They'd arrived in Styal as tradespeople, and their son William was a shoemaker. They wouldn't have wanted him to settle for the likes of an ex-workhouse brat. They certainly would have been appalled that she'd opened her legs for him within months of quitting the Apprentice House, presumably in a sluttish attempt to trap him into a hasty and unwelcome marriage and a room in the village. They must have stood their ground resolutely against the upstart Esther. This obduracy, and their physical separation, could explain much. Esther, according to the 1841 census, was living in the village anyway, at 5 Oak Cottages, with two other families, the Holts and the migrant Howletts, as portrayed in the second series of *The Mill.* William still lived with his family in Holts Lane. How frustrating for Esther, after all those years of fighting tooth and nail for what she wanted, for an identity, for the freedom to call something, or someone, her own; only to find her way barred by simple prejudice and obstinacy.

Couldn't they see she had risen above her beginnings? Didn't she deserve a chance at happiness with someone she obviously loved? Not with the Whittakers' son. The bond between Esther and William must have been strong to survive these times of separation. She was working her way through the mill, eventually becoming a weaver while bringing Thomas up as a single mother. There was an established wet-nursing network in the village of Styal throughout these times where some mothers, unable to work, would take in other girls' babies for a small sum, a practice taken up by the fictional Susanna Catterall.

Esther had seen off people tougher than Abraham and Esther Whittaker, and she seemed determined to outlast their objections. She couldn't have done this without William's support, going against his parents' wishes and sticking by her all that time. It also seems that he was unable to help Esther financially during this time. The mill's debt cash book of 1841 shows Esther borrowing £1 from one Jonathan Bailey. Paying for Thomas's day care must have made even greater demands on Esther's tight budget. Small wonder then that she pushed herself forward to scale greater heights of skill at work. I always have the feeling, whenever I consider Esther, that she must have felt that she would always have to prove herself. To prove her real age, prove she was top dog, prove she could outlast the apprentice system, prove she could learn to write, prove she could hold down a job and have a child, prove she could get herself a man with a trade and keep hold of him, prove that she was worthy of marriage to him too. She must have been a real force of nature and someone William was surely rightly proud of.

Further evidence of a continuing rift between Esther, William, young Thomas and William's parents is the date of their eventual wedding. Old Abraham outlived his wife and clung on until he was eighty-four and blind. You could imagine Esther cajoling William to get married anyway, what Abraham couldn't see, he wouldn't ever know about. They didn't, and Abraham duly popped his clogs in June 1851. Esther and William married in October of that year, and not at St Bart's either. Was it the last laugh on Esther's part that they were married at St Mary's, Stockport, a much 'posher' church than St Bart's and something that would definitely have got the collective goats of William's parents? No ordinary wedding for Esther, not St Bart's, where everyone and their dogs were baptised, married and buried, oh no, this was a grander affair, this was a 'look at me' affair. And who could blame her? What's more, by this time Esther had learned to write, or at least sign her name – her actual signature appears on the certificate. The couple's devotion to each other bore two more boys, William (again) and Abraham (it took four boys to deliver the name Abraham!).

Samuel Greg took a lot less time to get to the altar, but arguably overcame just as many hurdles. Although reputedly a charming man, Samuel was often tongue-tied and hesitant in his pursuit of Miss Hannah Lightbody of Liverpool. Hannah's diary and letters from that time tell us that she was not at all convinced that Samuel was the man for her. First impressions though, were favourable. In her diary for 12 November 1788, Hannah writes: 'Supped at Mr Kennedy's – met MR and Miss Greg – was much pleased with the latter and surprised I should never have heard of him before – sat by him all evening.' This is the first we ever hear of Hannah meeting Samuel and it doesn't take long before they meet again, one day in fact, and Samuel was quick off the mark. On 13 November Hannah writes: 'Went to the assembly. Mr and Mrs Philips made their appearance. Mrs I P fainted away – great confusion. Engaged to dance with Mr Philips. Mr Greg came and desired Mr Philips would let him dance with me – had a very pleasant evening.' By December they were meeting often, and on the 11th Hannah visits the assembly again, this time without the Philipses in tow. 'Went to the Assembly – danced again with Mr G. – very happy.' Three days later and they are exchanging notes. On 15 December Hannah has to leave Manchester to go home to Liverpool. She writes, 'Left Manchester with much regret.' Probably the first and last time she ever wrote those words. On 30 December, Hannah is back home: '. . . came home – found Mr Greg had been to Liverpool – much mollified. Went to the Concert – very uncomfortable – a trial of temper ill sustained.'

It seems from these early exchanges that both were quite smitten with each other; certainly Samuel seems to have the bit between his teeth. Hannah, however, was to rue this early haste. She begins to worry that she might be rushing into things with Samuel. I get the feeling that Hannah was prepared to take her time seeking out a suitable man to marry, and certainly did not even entertain most of the men she met at home – that 'troop of shallow brained fellows the Young men of Liverpool', as she called them. She remains suitably unimpressed, even when considering older men. 'Men I knew were in general, selfish and unreasonable and instead of being satisfied with and making the most of those excellencies a woman had they were apt to expect she should excel in everything.'

So, Hannah has set her bar high, and most men she meets fall way under it. Could it also be said that they were just as put off by her but for different reasons? She was bookish, impatient, probably a little pretentious and certainly strong-minded and unyielding. When Hannah met Samuel, could it have been a case of an immovable object meeting an irresistible force? Whenever I think of these two I am always reminded of *The Taming of the Shrew*, which is probably a little harsh, but the nagging feeling won't go away. High-minded Hannah clearly fell in love with this charming young Irishman a lot more quickly than she'd ever envisaged, and Samuel ardently pursued her, through letters and a flurry of arranged meetings in their first few months. The testy little entry in Hannah's diary of 30 December, where, by some quirk of fate, she and Samuel missed each other by days, is pinpointed by her biographer David Sekers as the moment she probably realised she was in love with him. On 5 January, Hannah recorded, 'Wrote to Manchester – and was much affected.' Sometimes it takes a perceived loss of something or someone to make you realise how much that person means to you and this is probably what happened to Hannah over this new year period between 1788 and 1789.

Samuel, not given to recording his thoughts too readily, is

not quoted on the subject of his marriage, but his letter to Hannah earlier in their courtship more than hints at his ardour. He complains that she is dithering over his proposal and even dangles the prospect of a rural idyll at Styal, knowing her love of nature, 'My delight is great in imagining future days, & the spot visited yesterday (QB) I regard as the seat of many promised joys.' He goes on to implore her to commit to him. 'Why will you insist on two lingering seasons & why make me impatient of the duration of an autumn which you can so peculiarly bless.' Tellingly, he begins this letter with a confession, 'Oh, how little justice my friends do me when they suppose me insensible to your merits, because my words are not loud in your praise.' Where he is expected to raise the roof with admiration as his friends pry, he 'can only answer them with a smile'.

By the end of January, though, there is a change in the atmosphere, 'a long conversation with Miss Cropper . . . long explanation in my room – was much distressed'. Then nothing for three months. Not a mention of Samuel as Hannah goes about her daily routines as if he'd never existed. Had someone, Miss Cropper perhaps, pointed out the chalk and cheese nature of them both? Had Hannah herself applied the brakes, after some romantic or social faux-pas by Samuel? Whatever the reason for this separation, by April Hannah is back in Manchester and suddenly Mr G is peppering the diary like a rash. By early November they are married. Hannah Lightbody has been swept off her feet, but not before a few last minute digging-in of heels . . .

It seems that Hannah has almost resigned herself to marrying

Samuel, but wakes up each morning with a list of queries and nagging questions that just won't go away. Her diary for 19 July has the following entry: 'A very unhappy morning with S.G. Walked to the park in the evening. Had a very pleasant walk, repeated poetry and became easy and tranquil.' Imagine Samuel, trying his damnedest to get Hannah down the aisle, and she's vexed with him and has to go off reading poetry to regain her equilibrium? The whole of July is taken up with the writing of letters to Mr G. The 8th of August arrives and so does Samuel, on horseback. 'Dined at Mrs Bunney's with the Hartopps. Mr G. came and rode home with us by moonlight.' He wasn't often around but when he was, he did it with some style.

Although by now the marriage must have been arranged, if not fixed, still Hannah vacillates. On 24 October, the wedding weeks away, 'Had a long painful conversation with Mr G. Sat with Mr Greg and read Paley.' A short description of what must have been, for Samuel, a long day indeed. David Sekers reveals the significance of this reading: 'If this is a reference to William Paley's *The Principles of Moral and Political Philosophy* published in 1785, then Samuel Greg must have been made fully aware of the serious and religious side of Hannah's character.' October was to prove a testing month for them both, literally in Samuel's case as Hannah put him through his moral and political paces. On 29 October, 'Sat up very late. Conversed with Mr G. upon objects of charity.' 30 October, 'Sat all morning with Mr G. Had a long and affecting conversation with him and was made happy.' 1 November: 'Mr G. sat with me all morning – thought on the entrance of this month of the event that was to take place in its course and prayed that it might make both S.G. and myself both happier and better.' The 'event that was to take place' being the marriage, hardly the most romantic of descriptions. But Samuel was not out of the woods just yet. Later that day, 'Disputed with S.G. about Homer's Iliad . . .' You can imagine Samuel, pleased that their morning chat had made them both 'happier and better', breathing a sigh of relief, pouring them both a celebratory cup of tea, only to get caught out by Homer. Hannah was relentless, 'was vexed to be so warm about it and secretly vowed not to hold any Arguments on such sort of subjects after I was married.' The word 'secretly' here holds another key. Hannah did not let Samuel off the hook by admitting to him that Homer was off the menu for their married life. He was left dangling, expecting ancient Greek philosophers to take him by surprise every time he opened a door. Four days later Hannah writes simply, 'Was married. May God bless with His favour this Connection and lead those who are engaged in it to more Virtue and Usefulness.' After this did we get an outpouring of emotion? The rest of the day's diary is as follows, 'Breakfasted at Park. Miss Cropper came from Everton to meet us. It snowed and rained very hard – found congratulatory notes when we got home – answered them. Was very busy and uncomfortable all the rest of the day.'

So, the courtship was over and the marriage began. How different all this was to the courtships of the apprentices, once into early adulthood. No letters, no billets-doux, no ruminations over Homer. Only wealthy people had the time and disposition to choose their future spouses carefully and with much consultation between friends and family. The working classes would mostly marry to start a family, though given the number of pregnant brides around, it was a question of sex first, proposal after (if at all – though it was the accepted thing. Maria Hough and Susanna Catterall must have been bitterly disappointed). Then the ensuing children would be put to work as soon as humanly possible, something the mills accommodated with alacrity. Still, most marriages lasted until death, usually the death of the husband. Then the widow would take off her mourning gown, dust down her best bonnet, and look out for someone to take on any children she had. It was a practical business, there were mouths to feed. Equally, a widowed man couldn't work with babies to take care of. He needed to find a new wife. It wasn't a case of what you wanted, it was more of what you needed. So, while the masters waxed lyrical about love, or at least some of them did, the workers got on with the dirty business of sex. More often than not, matches were made according to your needs, less about who actually took your fancy. If the two coincided, then you felt blessed.

Maybe apprentice-turned-overlooker Charlie Crout was blessed. The real one, that is, who unlike his fictional counterpart led a blameless life. There is a record of his marriage to Christiana Bayley at St Bart's Church in Wilmslow, on 25 June 1821. Christiana was a widow aged forty-seven when Charlie married her. He was twenty-six and had no children. She, it seems, was also childless, and well past the age of child-bearing. So, when they married, we can safely assume it wasn't for the purpose of child-bearing or child-minding. Could it be they actually married for love? I'd like to think so. Christiana died and was buried at St Bart's on 26 May 1832. Not having any children to tend to while working, Charlie didn't rush into another marriage. He waited until he met Hannah Toft, and they married on 18 February 1835 in Stockport. They went on to have three daughters, the first, Harriet, dying aged eleven months, and the last, Hannah, being born just a year before Charlie's death. Charlie died aged fifty, in 1845, a week before his and Hannah's fifteenth wedding anniversary. Needless to say, Charlie's widow, Hannah, remarried one Thomas Adshead and lived locally until her death aged sixty-seven in 1867. All are buried at St Bart's.

Elizabeth McGinn was certainly blessed, with a family of her own. The youngest of the Chelsea girls, whom we last saw leaving home on their way to the mill, had been left motherless at the age of three, and eventually had to be given up by her soldier father. She went on to work hard, and married a cotton spinner named William Garside in 1825, when she was twenty-three. No fewer than eight children followed: James, Thomas, Harriet, Edwin, Hannah, Elizabeth, Sarah and George. Elizabeth had beaten the odds: survived her desolate early life and surrounded herself with her brood of children, and then lived long enough to love and cherish them in a way that had been so cruelly denied to her.

At least when they left home for the mill, leaving their widowed father and little brother behind, the Bowden sisters had each other. They must have been model workers, never appearing in any of the stoppages ledgers for wrongdoings. Mary Bowden even won a prize. In 1840 she was given an award for 'good conduct', presented by none other than Robert Hyde Greg himself. She was presented with a Bible, a rare honour. Mary went one better than Elizabeth McGinn – she had nine children. The first was Thomas, born in 1844 and illegitimate. She later married the father, a carder named Jonathan Faulkner, in early 1845, and they went to live in the village, where Mary had the other eight children. In 1876, a year before she died, a photographic portrait of Mary as an adult was taken and appears on the cover of Keith Robinson's *Where Did They Come From?*. It's thought to be the only recorded image of any apprentice ever taken – another distinction for Mary.

Whether you were lucky in love was a lottery; no doubt not all unions matched the genuinely lifelong love affair between Esther and William. At least they were unions. There is a letter in the archives by Henry Russell Greg in 1863, which tells of an extremely unfortunate affair. Infuriatingly, the letter is both unfinished and undated, so we don't even know the recipient, but its contents speak for themselves. It tells us the story of John Knight, son of the gardener at Quarry Bank, someone who seemingly held the 'post of under bailiff and working factotum at Reddish'. John was further described thus: 'of a very reserved and jealous disposition though otherwise exceedingly respectable and a valuable servant'. It tells the recipient and us that John Knight had been 'courting some Hannah for three years'. This particular Hannah was reputedly from the nearby village of Prestbury, and, for whatever reason John had been 'past off by her'. Had his 'reserved and jealous' nature driven her away, after three years? Had she simply fallen in love with another man? Whatever the reason, John's reaction was final.

The letter begins: '. . . suicide Sunday morning in the reservoir above the mill at Quarry Bank'. John Knight had taken himself up to the lake, created to help power the mill, swam out to the middle, and allowed himself to sink into its muddy brown waters. Henry Greg writes on: 'all circumstances attending the suicide were so . . . deliberate that the verdict was "killed himself in the entire possession of his senses".' We know this is a legally appropriate term, but could John, so desperately seeking oblivion from his emotional pain that he chose such a terrible and public death, be rightly be described as possessing his senses? Greg continues: 'The girl does not seem in any way to blame,' and tells us, 'he was buries [sic] last night at Wilmslow without a service.' At this time, the act of suicide was still illegal, and males taking their own lives forfeited their worldly goods and inheritances, bringing social disgrace to the remaining members of their families. The church took a very dim view of those poor people who had been driven to suicide, viewing it as a crime against God, since, in the very act of killing yourself, you had given up your faith in God's mercy. As a result of this thinking, churches also stated that suicides could not be buried in daylight hours, deeming it permissible only between nine o'clock in the evening and midnight. It wouldn't be until 1882 that those who died by their own hand were allowed a daylight burial. It is also said that the bodies of those committing suicide would be buried under the walls of the church grounds so that no one visiting the church could walk over the graves. Henry Greg's sorrowful letter trails off in an awful postscript: 'It has nearly killed his mother . . .'

Chances of finding their one true love, or failing that a decent steady man, were narrowed down for Quarry Bank girls once the Gregs adopted the policy of only accepting female apprentices. They'd tired of dealing with recalcitrant boys and young men. As the gap grew between the newer girls coming into the apprentice house, and the ages of the working men already there, any chance of finding anybody started to dwindle into the distance. Girls seeking a partner would have had to look at the wider community around Styal, and perhaps those walks into Wilmslow on a Sunday took on a new meaning and were undertaken with greater urgency and hope. Certainly romantic opportunities were not to be passed up lightly.

Although we have no spoken record of how the likes of Esther, Susanna and Maria felt about love and sex, we do have testimony from the Oral Histories, still sitting in the mill archives. In these recordings we can hear those very voices, crackling with emotion as the memories are dredged up from the past. Emily Lyons, an apprentice at the turn of the twentieth century, almost whispers when responding to the interviewer's question about sex and the facts of life:

'No one told me . . .'

'But you knew what to expect?'

'Oh, yes . . .' she wistfully replied.

So Emily had heard that train, all whistles and bells, thundering down the track.

Whereas Emily was one of those seemingly helpless in the path of the train, I get the feeling that Bertha Brown fancied herself as the driver. Bertha (née Silverwood) worked in the mill as a young girl during the early 1900s, and also recorded her memories. She says that she was once cornered by two boys who wanted her to go for a 'walk' with them for they had 'heard what she was like by Florrie Downs'. Bertha didn't go for that walk, not on that day anyway, and the boys probably drifted off back to Florrie Downs. Would she have found love, or just the sex? Bertha, who turned out to be a latter-day Esther Price, would never know.

One thing Bertha did know, however, was how to get away with treating the Gregs with a remarkable lack of respect, as we shall see. This particular girl had enough sass for a whole village, yet was her behaviour just a direct result of the way in which the Gregs treated their workers? To begin with, Bertha had never known the hardships of the Apprentice House, having lived in the village, itself a construct of and monument to the Gregs' paternalistic fiefdom.

She'd not known the deprivation of the parentless apprentices, who would have gazed longingly at those fellow workers trudging off in their intact family units to their very own homes in the village. Esther before her had seen social elevation to the village as something desirable, something people with families did, people with parents and a glimpse of some future. For many of the child apprentices, though, the village was to prove elusive, and the few dozen yards between the Apprentice House and thos ein the village might as well as have been the distance to the other side of the world. For those who attained it, life in the village meant they'd arrived. But arrived where exactly and with what consequences?

The village at Quarry Bank is as unique as the people it has housed for over two centuries. It still stands today, fully populated, and its cobbled streets echo to the whispers of generations. Listen to our stories, the whispers go, marvel at our lives.

CHAPTER NINE

The Village

The village at Styal was, and still is, unique. It was born out of a drive to attract, recruit and house itinerant workers to a rural setting, away from the more densely populated powerhouse settings for cotton mills, the cities. But pioneering industrialist Samuel Greg did not actually invent the village of Styal in its entirety. We can trace the village back some years before Samuel first clapped eyes on where he was to live most of his adult life, and where he was to die. Back almost three hundred years.

In the year 1331 the areas around Wilmslow were being developed for a basic form of farming. An early charter, dated 1331, mentions the village by name: 'To all . . . John, son of Edmund Ffiton, parson of the church of Wilmslow a piece of my land at Stiale in Pownale for erecting there a certain grange for the tenth of corn of the said Hugh.'

So a document drawn up for the basis of a tithe rent gives us our first glimpse of the name, albeit spelt differently. In a document printed during the early twentieth century by Reg Worthington, a lifelong inhabitant of the village and exmillworker, there is unearthed evidence of how the village further developed. Seemingly further grants by Edmund Ffiton name a place in Stiale called Curbishley. This area eventually gave its name to a family which in itself can be traced through many generations. During the reign of Henry VIII, a document recording an action taken by a Hugh Curbishley against a John Carte and his wife Agnes names the village as Styall. Curbishley was trying to recover properties belonging to him, a mess, a toft, two cottages, their gardens and 43 acres of land. So the Styall of Henry's reign was worth fighting over. By 1577 the village had become 'the centre of a thriving rural community' with its own market. Thriving farming communities created work, work created wealth, wealth stimulated growth. Styall was expanding, drawing people in. People looking for land to farm and exploit. Some of Styall's indigenous population were in for a shock. The old practices that had provided locals with work began to die away; crop-growing and peat-cutting became obsolete, dragging families out from their roots. As new farmsteads and thatched houses cropped up all over the area, some families emerged into the light. A Mr Samuel Finney of Fulshaw Hall, Wilmslow, often referred to the area, which he clearly knew well. Finney tells of one such family, apparently and thrillingly for historians, leaving an abode all too familiar with anyone scouting the Greg gardens. He refers to 'a cavern in soft rock partly natural and partly artificial about four or five yards in compass each way the whole front of it is open . . . situated close upon the back of the River Bollin in a very retired narrow deep valley overhung with large beech and other trees . . .'

This almost perfectly describes the sandstone cave overlooking the Greg gardens, which fits snugly into the red rock to the north of Quarry Bank House. Finney continues: 'I think it was formerly a hermitage or religious retirement and abode of one Disley a devout hermit from whence it might obtain the name Disley kirk or church.' For someone, like myself, having lived in Disley, this is fascinating stuff. It gets better, or worse, depending on where you're coming from, 'I remember a poorman of the name of Murral with his wife and seven children living in it for many years, having made it habitable by filling up the front with gorse to keep out the cold.'

This was where I began to doubt that the Greg cave could be the same one as described by Finney. The location fits, back of the Bollin, surrounded by beeches . . . but *seven* children and two adults? Well, I hope not, for their sakes. The Greg cave isn't the only cave hewn from the soft red walls of the valley, perhaps there were others, cut deeper into the cliff and substantially better suited for living purposes? But the very fact of the original hermitage gives us a further idea of exactly how remote the early Styall was.

By the time the effects of the historic land-grabbing were beginning to be keenly felt in the area, in the middle of the eighteenth century, Styal was beginning to show some wear and tear. Whereas, when relatively prosperous, the local folk had thrived, they hadn't prepared, financially or mentally, for any downturn. According to Mr Finney, they were 'sixty years behind the times when compared with Yorkshire'. Ironically, given the enterprise shown later by Samuel Greg, Finney attributed this decline to 'a lack of boldness, they had lost the capacity to initiate'. Finney went further, apportioning the blame directly on drink and the subsequent slide into 'laziness'. He complained that locals 'had become a drunken quarrelling lot often found milling around ale houses'. Of which, in Styal, there were plenty. Dotted around the village green were the Horse Shoe Inn, the Mulberry Bush, the Royal Oak, the King William, the Queen Mary and the Ship Inn. Finney felt this was becoming unhealthy and that the people were becoming too 'inwardly looking'.

For most of Quarry Bank's life the land was rented by the Gregs from local landowner and aristocrat Lord Stamford, and the lordly declarations made doubly sure the booze was kept flowing. In one of Lord Stamford's many written stipulations regarding his land dealings with Samuel Greg, it is stated that Greg was 'to send any grain to be ground at the mills owned by Lord Stamford and to pay the accustomed dues for grounding there of . . . or to pay two shillings for every gallon of liquor of ale or any other liquors from malt, corn, grain that shall not be ground at the mill'. So, with dissolution on their doorstep, something had to give. Finney felt Styal had hit rock bottom as gangs roamed the countryside, 'Fearings and Braggarts lurking in every dark hole and hollow though they were just and honest to their equals they think it no crime to make free with the property of their superiors. To be betrayed by one of their equals was a scandalous crime.'

Finney set about finding work for those idle hands, and his prayers were answered by the introduction of silk-button-making in nearby Macclesfield. A fashion for silk rather than metal buttons couldn't have arrived at a better time. Agents representing Yorkshire woollen mills arrived scouting for 'putters out'. This was an early version of outsourcing and locals were encouraged to take up spinning in their homes. Things went well and Finney was satisfied, 'There were few houses in the village where the wheel is not going. Young people could earn twopence, threepence or fourpence a day.' So, Styal had its very own cottage industry, perfect for Samuel Greg to descend upon and utilise. Samuel favoured the 'putting out' system anyway, having many weavers scattered over Derbyshire for this very purpose. To find them on his new doorstep must have been encouraging.

In all of Samuel's business dealing, those with Lord Stamford showed Samuel at his worst, his least decisive. He drove his sons mad, especially Robert Hyde. Samuel's first lease with Lord Stamford was dated 1784, and it wasn't until 1828–9 that Samuel, pressed in the main by Robert Hyde, began negotiations with Lord Stamford to buy all the lands, including his recently formed 'village' in Styal. Lord Stamford offered the lot for what was considered a low price, at £58,915. After further consideration, another £3,728 was added for Morley Farms. This included Lord Stamford's calculation of the timber involved in the deal to be worth £5,500. A total of £62,643. Samuel baulked at the price, even though he himself valued the timber alone at over £10,000. Samuel set out to draw together his own valuation for the sale, which, after some months and stretching everyone's patience, unsurprisingly came in some several thousands under Lord Stamford's figure. It would have been daylight robbery and the aristocrat was having none of it. Robert Hyde stepped in and remonstrated with his father at the absurdity of the amount. Proud Samuel gave in and, that same day, offered Lord Stamford the asking price. He was rather rudely turned down. Samuel had dithered for nine months, unable to make the decision that he thought would 'make himself a poor man for life'. It wasn't until 1855 that Robert Hyde was able to buy the land. But then, in Samuel's defence, Lord Stamford could have been a difficult landlord in the way only English aristocrats could be. One of the many stipulations made on Samuel, enabling him to lease the land, was that 'he shall keep one hound, pointer or spaniel dog as shall from time to time be sent to the hunt'.

Despite his reluctance to buy the very land his whole business was founded on, Samuel forged ahead adapting it to his use. The farm buildings that his young children had probably played in during their holidays at Oak Farm were transformed into separate dwellings. Between 1785 and 1790 every building that could be adapted, was, resulting in over forty houses, with cellars. Initially the cellars were constructed to provide space for hand looms, but the increase in both new families coming to Styal and the expansion of those already there meant these cellars were used as 'overspill' space, often for the children of larger families, or young couples. In the television series both Esther Price and the Howlett family find themselves almost cheek by jowl in these cottages. For some it was their first home, and we see the fictional Esther's glee at being the mistress of her own space after all those years sharing cots with her fellow apprentices. For the Howletts, fictional and real, this made the difference from what was virtually a mud hut to a house built of bricks and with a roof. Standing in a cellar today at No 13 Oak Cottages and feeling its damp walls pressing in on you, it is difficult to share that enthusiasm. Admittedly, this cellar hasn't seen an inhabitant for over fifty years, but you can still feel the presence of people. People who were born in here, swaddled in rags, suckled in here and cut their first tooth. No larger than ten or twelve feet square, with one fly-blown window revealing no more than the steps that would taken them on their way to the mill, and which they would have staggered down at the end of the exhausting day.

On the day I stand there, the cold compresses you and your breath clouds in the still air. On hot days this must have hummed like an oven. The four peeling walls encompassing the whole spread of people's lives. Their loves, their children and their deaths. Mothers may well have stumbled down those same work-bearing steps with the laying-out board, borrowed from outside the village shop in the case of bereavement. Menfolk and children could well have been mourned in this very space, the wails of the grief-stricken bouncing off the walls and carrying up the steps and out across the fields. Were they ever loud enough to be heard at the Apprentice

House? Probably too far, even on a still day. You turn away from this room and climb the steps, shaking the warmth back into your bones and blowing the stale air from your lungs. Relieved that it wasn't you who had lived there and were grateful for the privilege.

In the same way that the village shop, originally owned and run by the Gregs, eventually became a co-operative, the workers were also encouraged to join the sick club. As its name suggests, this was an early form of medical insurance, founded around 1817, and financed by contributions from the workers, augmented with occasional grants from the mill. The rules of the sick club were revised in 1840, and a quick look down the list of stewards and officials throws up some familiar surnames. Sarah Henshall was a steward, John Tongue was the clerk and a certain John Waterworth is named as treasurer. Names that were beginning to resonate throughout the mill's history, beginning to take an active part in its future. In 1840, for the grand sum of half a farthing per each shilling of your weekly wage, you became a member. A member, that is, if you had attained the age of thirteen or were a man. Women in the village apparently belonged to another society, formed in 1827, learning to look after themselves. On production of a medical certificate after a week's absence from work, any member could hope to receive half wages for no more than twelve weeks. If you died, the benefits were anything ranging from £1 to £10 according to the seniority of your membership and the amount of your weekly contributions. So mercifully, and at a cost, gone were the days when your own funeral expenses, or those of a deceased parent, were deducted from whatever money you had saved or had to earn.

As with many co-operative agreements, where you would expect people in the same boat to behave with consideration to each other, there were teething problems. Reg Worthington recalls an anecdote with a salutary lesson for anyone thinking they were more equal than the others:

> Committee men acting as stewards gave them a sense of power which they exercised by enforcing benefit rules with a degree of stringency. This sometimes led to sickness benefits being withheld for petty infringements of the 'Rule Book.' This drew stewards and memberships apart since they appeared to rank above them instead of existing in one another's being. On occasions their attitude produced occasional unexpected responses as this following anecdote relates.

From this point on Reg quotes from the original source:

> Friday afternoon would find J . . . collecting rather pompously 'sick club' money during working hours. The week previously he caught a young operative reading a comic paper; he seized it and in a trance the paper went flying through the open window. A week later determined to pay off an old score, J . . .'s club book was pounced upon and thrown through the window whence it fell into the River Bollin. According

to allegorical [sic] accounts it floated down the stream and passed out of sight before J . . .'s unbelieving eyes. It was never recovered nor were the arrears and to add to the gratification of the membership the steward's self image had been deflated.

Some of these ex-apprentices would never forget where they came from, even if they lived in the village now, or at least not all of them would, although some ex-apprentice women had been known to prefer to have their own children schooled away for those 'workhouse brats', in the Apprentice House. It's human nature to want your children to have more than you had, even if it occasionally makes you forget what made you what you are.

Although Samuel had already supplied a school teacher for the Apprentice House, he felt the mounting pressure from his growing community to provide further education for the workers' children, outside the Apprentice House system. In 1820 he and Hannah founded the Oak School, still there today and still serving the children of the area. Samuel was twenty years ahead of the Compulsory Education Act of 1870. He was steadily learning that there was more to growing your own workforce than he had probably originally envisaged.

The same sort of social pressure resulted in the building and forming of the Methodist church and community in Styal. Samuel's people wanted to worship; why make them travel, wasting precious hours away from the mill and its village? They had a school, they could have a church. And ultimately, they all had a house, even if it was shared. Whereas millworkers in Manchester might expect to share a cellar with another twenty to thirty souls, Styal cottages often housed no more than seven or eight. Where there were larger families, they spilled over into other cottage cellars, sharing the load and the rent. Let's not pretend this was anything less than cold, cramped and fusty, but it was a home. Most cottages were two up, two down, with a cellar and a yard. It is true that wages at Quarry Bank were lower than those achievable in the cities, but so was the rent, cottages in Styal costing between one and two shillings per week. Apparently, when the mill worked short-time, as was often the case when it relied solely on water power, workers were not charged full rent.

So what did it cost to live in the village for an average young family in the mid-nineteenth century. Document No. 14 from the Quarry Bank archive holds an answer. This is an account of how people lived one week at a time and is authored by a Thomas Yates:

> This an account of the weekly expenditure and income of one member of witness's family delivered in on oath 27th July 1833.
>
> For a father, mother and two children for one week:

	£ s d
30lb loaf of bread	0 4 2
8lb of beef	0 4 4
20lb of potatoes	0 0 10
3lb of butter	0 3 0

3½lb sugar	0 1 9
2oz tea	0 0 7½
2oz coffee	0 0 2½
3lb flour	0 0 6
12 oatcakes	0 1 0
7 quarts ale	0 2 11
7 quarts milk	0 1 6
1lb soap	0 0 6
½lb candles	0 0 3
Rent	0 3 6
Washing	0 2 4
Fire	0 1 0
	£1 8 5

Earnings per week in family - £2 10 0

This is an account of the expenditure and income of a man and his wife, both of them are spinners, furnished to me by Thomas Yates, who collected the particulars from the man and not the woman; he applied to the man, Matthew . . . because he believed him to be the one who would tell the truth. 27th July 1833.

Thomas Yates then goes on to add another list which shows a total expenditure of £12s 1½d against a joint wage of £2 10s 0d for a childless couple, provided the untrustworthy woman hadn't nobbled her husband in the first place. The ingredients are almost identical; it's only the amounts that differ. No coffee for this couple, opting for bacon instead. Also, at 3 quarts, they claim to be drinking less than half the married couple's amount of ale. Is this what the other couple found having children did to them, drove you to drink, or did the disingenuous wife actually have a quiet word with the honest husband – whatever you do, don't let them think we're drunks? Presumably the money left over would have gone towards the luxuries – shoes, bonnets, underwear – maybe even a blowout during Wakes' Week? I'm sure Matthew and his good lady wife needn't have worried unduly about the amount they drank each week. Who hasn't, when faced with the modern-day doctor's question of how many 'units' you currently imbibe, been economical with the truth? Drinking was rife and didn't necessarily stop anyone from achieving positions of trust. Step forward James Kinsey, who succeeded James Henshall (another one!) as mill manager in 1867. Kinsey, according to the mill memoranda, was described as 'plausible enough and knew fairly about machinery but turned out very ordinary and indifferent and not steady or sober'. James became known colloquially as 'Pisspot Kinsey'. On 15 September 1885, the mill memoranda records, 'James Kinsey who had been manager since March 1867 was taken suddenly ill and after lingering in an unconscious state until the 17th died.' There is a sobering addendum, 'Was a fool for the last 2 or 3 years.'

And so the community thrived, even as the fortunes of the cotton industry fluctuated and the masters changed. Factory workers patrolled the streets armed with billy clubs during the Plug Riots (of which more in the next chapter). The shop evolved, eventually selling more than basic groceries. Shoes, hats and even underwear appeared in the windows. You could grow your own food. You were taught, you could worship. You could nip down to the local pub, if you were a man, and start a fight with that weaver who'd had a go at you for what he said was uneven weft. Some years you even had as many as six days' holidays – nowhere to go, mind, but the days were there. You had everything you needed; not necessarily what you desired, but who did, apart from the masters? And, what's more, you never had to leave the village for any of it. Cradle to grave all within the few acres of land. Some would leave Styal only in a box, on a cart and with their loved ones trailing behind, on foot, all the way to St Bart's. So the community tended to look inwards, something their predecessors had been accused of before. Everyone knew everyone else's business, which wasn't always a good thing.

And, among the most knowledgeable of those in the village seems to have been Thomas Tonge, whose recollections, we have already discovered, throw up some memorable characters. There are many people today whose ancestors served their time in the cotton mills of the north who are blissfully unaware of their heritage, and there are equally many hungry for this knowledge. Sometimes all it takes is to see a name, ask a question (or a few), and it all comes tumbling out. The Gregs, Henshalls, Crouts, Whittakers, Prices, Waterworths, Worthingtons, Wrights; all have reasons to look back in dismay, amazement and pride. As the archive continues to be plumbed for its still-kept secrets, more of the following names and stories will be revealed. Tonge's document deserves close attention for, like Quarry Bank, it is also a unique record of times, characters and dialect.

Matthew Boon appears fictionally in the second series of the television adaptation of Quarry Bank's story and ironically, it seems, he could have appeared in the show had it been made then. Tonge recalls: '(Prentice) overlooker, the leading character at all the Christmas theatricals, taking "Shylock" in Merchant of Venice, "Sir Peter Teazle" in School for Scandal, and similar roles.' Matthew was also something of a reciter and vocalist at parties and was reputedly known for his most popular pieces, 'Ye crags and peaks' and his song, 'Cork Leg'. So the community had even got around to providing their own entertainment, and Matthew, it seems, was their star.

Whereas the Gregs had always sought to bring the outside world into the village, usually in the shape of visiting speakers and debaters, often their own offspring, the village sometimes seems to be keeping the world at arm's length. When Robert Hyde Greg stood in front of the rebellious crowd of would-be rioters during the Plug Riots, he blamed the situation on fools 'tippling in ale houses'. In other words, as far as his own workers were concerned, nothing to do with us, nothing to see here. Ignore them and they'll go away, we look after our own. Had Robert Hyde himself become one of the inward-lookers, something he may have even accused his late father of being? Something that Samuel Finney had accused the earlier inhabitants of being? Even if Finney was right, the village could still throw up fascinating characters.

Two such characters would have often been at each others'

throats. There were three Broadhursts in Styal in Thomas Tonge's time. Two were respectable father and son, Charles and William. The third was not so respectful, another William. This William Broadhurst was an elderly millhand, living in the village with his family, described as comprising 'Charles – died in Egypt, Joseph, John, William, Samuel, Henry and daughters'. Note the daughters don't even get a namecheck. William had a nickname, 'Hag', and was a poacher of note. Those local lads either brave enough or simply not close enough to get clipped would sing at William when they saw him, 'Hag, Hag, Hag, three rappits in a bag'. You could be fairly sure Hag wouldn't have wanted his reputation bandied around in a song in such public places as the village green, and chances are the lads would have at least received many a brooding glare for their impudence. God save them then if they underestimated Hag's turn of speed, especially for one so relatively old.

Poaching was a serious business, and it had only been as recently as 1816 that poachers were no longer hanged for this offence. After that date, they could have expected at least a goodly spell in Australia, as much as fourteen years, if they made it back at all. Whereas before land enclosure poachers were seen universally as vermin, thieves either too greedy or too lazy to work for a living and rear their own game, attitudes changed after the Enclosure Acts. Now, some folk saw poachers as the most noble of criminals, only taking from the wealthy unscrupulous landowners what by rights had always been theirs anyway. The Robin Hoods of the rural communities. The landowners didn't see it this way and never had. Once hanging was no longer an option as far as a deterrent was concerned, they sought other means. If you could not or did not want to stay up all night, every night, protecting your land, there were other means of deterring these men. Guns were wedged between tree roots and spring-guns were used that, once triggered, would aim to mutilate, maim or break the poachers' legs. Of course, if the guns were accidentally wedged in aiming too high, or had slipped somewhat during the night – or even been dislodged by the poachers themselves – then all bets were off. The death of a poacher was not unknown, and, after all, they brought it on themselves. James Sparkes and his merry bunch of boys must have really wanted Farmer Dale's apples badly. During the 1830s these horrible traps and guns were outlawed, but the long voyage to the other side of the world still beckoned for anyone still sneaking through the woods at night with several sacks tucked into their belts. How Hag must have hated those lads.

John Brown, on the other hand, would have welcomed a chat with old Hag. As the Gregs' gamekeeper, it's not inconceivable that Brown knew all about Hag but had yet to catch him. The position of gamekeeper meant Brown was a trusted member of the Greg entourage and would often be seen in the company of his masters. Tonge's recollection of Brown is less about him and more about his relationship with the Gregs. They clearly had a sense of humour. Brown apparently lodged with Frank Scott and 'Old Mrs Scott'. Frank's wife is not given her Christian name. Old Mrs Scott was known for being able to 'swear fluently and forcefully'. Tonge takes up the story:

> One day she had made a big potato pie to last her folks two dinners, along with other things. Her folks had their dinner and returned to work. She lay down in the parlor for a nap prior to 'siding up'. Brown and two or three of the Gregs, after shooting all forenoon, getting as hungry as hunters, called at Scotts on their way to Norcliffe, found Mrs Scott asleep, ate the remaining half of the potato pie and all the other food on the table and then took their seats on a bench outside the front door, to wait results. Mrs Scott woke up and on missing the food 'swore like a trooper', rushed to the front door where she found the thieves laughing, whereupon she was profuse in her excuses, but she had given them a fine sample of what she could do in the line of cursory remarks.

Brown seems like someone you could reason with, someone with a relaxed manner. Perhaps he and Hag came to a gentlemen's agreement and many a blind eye was turned? Or maybe Hag had more sense than to poach so close to home?

The Davenport family were quite prominent in the village. Old Isaac Davenport was a carter who used two-wheel carts to fetch cotton from Broadheath and took finished cloth to Manchester. This had been his father, Jonathan's, work also. Isaac had grown-up sons and daughters by his first wife, presumed dead, and stepchildren and a new child by his new wife, who was 'a Baguley from the Romplin' Kitlin'. In other words, she was from nearby Ringway. One of Isaac's grown-up sons, and Isaac's brother, are described thus in Tonge's recollections:

> ISAAC DAVENPORT, millhand, not married, one of the sons of old Isaac, sex uncertain, good laundress, somewhat feminine voice, very much in evidence in 'May Singing' and 'Christmas Singing'; nick-name 'Margit'.
> JOHN DAVENPORT, brother of old Isaac, farm labourer, lived past the Horse Shoe on the Handforth road, nick-name 'Foo Dameput', married, no children.

The not-so veiled allusions to the men's sexuality is interesting. Clearly, in Isaac Jnr's case he was not about to hide his light under any bushels and, nickname apart, doesn't seem to have been given any reason to. Was the Greg's liberalism filtering down to such a degree that it was encouraging tolerance of all walks of life? Isaac's uncle John, although married, must have displayed some sort of behaviour to earn his own unique nickname. Perhaps the village did close ranks and look after its own? To such a degree that no one was excluded or isolated, regardless of race, creed, religion and sexual persuasion? If so, a remarkable achievement indeed. Tonge remembers the Howlett family too. He could well have been there when the Howletts pitched up in their rags, filthy and exhausted from their journey to this new world. He introduces John Howlett: 'native of Buckinghamshire, old, one of McLaren's labourers; had a worthless son – Jack an several daughters.' This was at a time when John Howlett was probably considered ill suited to continue in the mill in any way and, after a fashion, ended up where he began, working the land. John's wife comes out of this anecdote well:

> His wife Mary, a big, fat woman, not a bad sort, was a character. In his later days he was querulous and complaining. One night John awoke his wife, saying, 'Meary, Meary, I am a dyin'.' She had heard that sort of thing before more than once, so merely replied, 'All right, John, get on wi' thy dyin' and I will cry for thee in the mornin', I am going to sleep', which she did.

Tonge also knows William Whittaker, Esther Price's husband and father to her children. But he apparently doesn't know him that well. Tonge says of William: 'WILLIAM WHITTAKER, shoe maker, lived in cottage between Farm Fold and the Ship, had a step-son – Thomas Price.' This is a fundamental misunderstanding. Thomas Price was William's second-born son by Esther, the first, also William, having died in infancy. The 1861 census tells us that William and Esther were, indeed, living at Farm Fold. They were both aged forty-one and had Thomas (named as Whittaker) aged seventeen and Abraham aged six with them. Esther did not survive long after the census, dying in November of that year. Was it because Esther lived so long as a single mother with Thomas that people assumed he wasn't William's? People certainly had their opinion of Esther the troublemaker, why not Esther the hussy? And, anyway, Thomas was known as a Price, only taking the name Whittaker after his mother was married to William. And, sure enough, Thomas pops up again in a census. This time he appears in the 1871 census as Thomas Price, aged twenty-seven, and his wife Martha, aged twenty-two. They have two sons, John aged four years and George, aged four months. Thomas's occupation is registered as 'mule spinner in cotton mill'. Could it be that folk had always assumed that Thomas wasn't William's son? The older William's parents, the formidable Esther and Abraham, thought so little of their son's choice of girlfriend they may well not have disabused people of this notion. Maybe Thomas himself was unimpressed by the manner of his father's seeming 'abandoning' of Esther by living with his parents while she struggled with him as a baby? Hence the shift in name. Or perhaps he disagreed with his father's haste in remarrying Eliza Barrow? Whatever the circumstances, the normally intuitive and keen-eyed Thomas Tonge slipped up with the Prices.

The Henshalls practically have a whole page of recollections to themselves, but then again, there was more than one strand of Henshalls. Tonge divides them tribally. The Henshalls born of George the warper and the Henshalls born of Peter the joiner are from 'The Valley of the Weaver', and are not related to the Henshalls of Styal. The 'Valley of the Weaver' reference, although sounding like some 1960s potboiler about the dubious practices of the weaving profession, does in fact, simply mean that they came from by the River Weaver. One Henshall attracted some unwanted attention and had a nickname that even the garrulous Tonge daren't spell out

> THOMAS HENSHALL, one of the three joiners at the mill, sometimes called 'Joiner Thomas' to distinguish him from his namesake cousin 'Warper Thomas'. Had sons – Alfred, Arthur and Peter and Daughters. Nick-name – unprintable, but expressing his fawning sycophancy to any one above him. Not popular with young people; he seemed to have forgotten he was ever young himself. On favourable occasions, in the dusk or evening, was well snow-balled, without discovering the offenders, who took care to plaster his face and ears with snow balls first – 'the young dogs' as he called them.

The village was a religious place where, apart from the established church of the Unitarians, Norcliffe, and the Methodists' Chapel, there were many meetings in cellars and the like, when visiting preachers would ply their religious trade. Tonge's list contains a George Sumner, and with it a peek at how some of these preachers were perceived:

> GEORGE SUMNER, millhand, Farm Fold, prominent among local Primitive Methodists, who held services in 'Ranter's Cellar', near Marble Bank. Had two sons – Robert (who robbed the Missionary Box of the Methodist Chapel and was afterwards named 'Missionary Bob') and John and one daughter.

So, 'Ranter's Cellar' was how some described the where and how of preaching, and the family's fear of God did not extend to being afraid of stealing from Him. Notice, again, the afterthought of a daughter.

Another Sumner, William, gets a mention, although it's his second wife who catches the eye.

> His second Wife Sarah (much younger than he was) was a good natured but excitable woman with a loud voice. She wore 'for best' a capacious bonnet, of the style then known as 'Cottage', black satin outside lined with white satin. One Sunday as the congregation left the Methodist Chapel, they were startled by loud exclamations from Sarah Sumner inside her own house. Some of them went to the door to inquire what was the matter and were tearfully told by Sarah – 'A'ar owd cat has gone an' kitted in my best bonnet!'

Wives were a constant source of amusement for some of the gentlemen of the village. It would seem that the lifetime of hard labour had not dulled everyone's sense of humour. I suppose sometimes that things got so dark, there was nothing else to do but to laugh.

> SAMUEL MOORES, laborer at Oak Farm, elderly, lived in Back Row in Village, posed as a clock mender, invented a primitive alarm clock, nick-name, 'Sammy Larum'. For a second wife married Mary Sumner, elderly spinster, who, by reason of spinal trouble, was not much more than four feet high, but

> nearly the same in width. Walter Turner lent his 'shandry' to drive to church to be married. The women of the village turned out to see the bridal pair depart. James Gratrix observed – 'Aw dun-no what owd Sammy intends to do wi' her, but if aw were him aw'd sit her wi' duck eggs.'

However, some of the villagers weren't in the least amusing and the following inhabitant must have been a terrifying prospect for all of the apprentice children.

> JOHN JACKSON, farm labourer, brother of Charles and James, not married, a big man, in drink the 'village bully', made his headquarters with his sisters at the Prentice House, where they did the laundry work for Norcliffe and Quarry Bank.

So, every village has one, only this one was another pure Dickensian. It must have been terrifying to have Jackson based around the Apprentice House anyway, but when we learn of where he slept, the horror intensifies: 'He was reputed to sleep in the pig cote.' So not only did the apprentices have to face him lurking around all day, they had to contend to the sight of this 'big man' rising from sleeping with the pigs. The very fact that he did so says something about his mental health and his disposition. Here was someone so base that they did not care either what others thought of them, or indeed, what they thought of themselves. Someone who enjoyed the power their physical presence had over others and someone who was prone to bouts of violence. Someone without those social parameters these days would probably be qualified as a sociopath. Add in the toxic mix of alcohol and you have a time bomb. The girls must have walked back to the Apprentice House in bunches or at least in twos and stayed well away from the pig cote, especially after dark.

As is often the case with large, dangerous predators, it can be the small things that bring them down. Jackson was employed by one Walter Turner to look after his turnips that were growing in the fields adjacent to the Apprentice House. You can imagine the locals not really knowing what to do with such a man as Jackson. Keep him out of harm's way, harming other people, that is. Keep him away from the Ship Inn. Appeal to his family to exert some form of control. It's interesting that he didn't seem to be living with either his brothers or sisters, maybe they wouldn't have him. If you have a volatile nature, it isn't necessarily going to be cowed just because you're related, they were probably just as afraid as anyone else. So, out in the open fields, where everyone can see you and with plenty of distance in between, seemed the best place for him. It is also a measure of his mental faculties that this work was best suited to him. He didn't need to think, he just needed to be there, a huge physical presence. What could go wrong? If you are paid by your master to guard something, in this case turnips, what is the worst thing you could do? What could you possibly not get away with? Sure enough, one day Walter Turner himself caught Jackson stealing the very turnips he was being paid to guard. How did he try and explain any turnips that had gone missing before? Thieves outwitted him? He didn't see them across the empty expanse of the fields? Perhaps they were just too quick for him? Whatever excuse he'd given, Turner showed up one day to see for himself and caught the only possible thief it could have been in the act. Before he could face the law, Jackson fled. I don't believe the apprentices didn't still fear him though. He was now on the run and more desperate than ever. They must have huddled together more tightly than ever as they hurried down the road in the dark, starting at every twitch of a branch or rustle in the hedgerows. Sometimes it is only the victims of a bully who really know what their abuser is capable of. Others can only guess. In reality, for however he remained at large, he was eventually discovered. Tonge tells us: 'he absconded and finally died at Burnage. Even he had a good side to him.'

So, only in his death did Jackson ever do anything that the village approved of.

Not all drunks were given to violence. Some went peacefully about their business, bothering no one and earning the protective actions of the community. Such a man was George Shaw and the following tale must have seemed like a normal Saturday night to him:

> GEORGE SHAW, elderly, bald, farm labourer, not married, a character, always good natured, illiterate, with education would have made his mark, addicted to

> drink. One Sunday morning boys found him lying on the pavement on Horse Lane. Sleeping off his Saturday night drunk. As George awoke and sat up, John Waterworth and Thomas Hewitt (two leading Methodists) arrived. John Waterworth said, in the style all his own, 'George my lad, George my lad, whatever will become of thee?' Thomas Hewitt, in his austere style, said, 'George, the devil will get you.' To the entertainment of the boys, George replied, 'An' suppose he does. I never did the devil any harm and he won't do me any harm; it's folks such as you, that are always backbitin' him, that he'll turn over with his fork for further roastin'.' The two Methodists left and the boys helped George to his feet and started him towards his Sister's house in the village.

I suspect Waterworth and Hewitt turned the other cheek the next time they found George on their way to chapel. There is one other example of how people's attitudes towards the religious folk in the village was not always harmonious. These inhabitants of Styal clearly had minds and opinions of their own, something that Unitarian and liberal Hannah would have mightily approved of and, indeed, encouraged her whole life at Styal. However, though she encouraged free thought, she might not have always approved of the methods of delivery. Robert Brierley was a 'roller coverer' at the mill and lived in School Row with two sons and the ubiquitous gaggle of unnamed daughters. Although he was, according to Tonge, 'a peculiar character in various ways', it is what happened to his mother that catches the eye:

> His mother, Ellen Brierley, a dear old woman and Methodist of the old type, lived in a two room (one up and one down) cottage called 'Brook Hall', opposite the Oak Farm gate, which cottage was pulled down years ago. She had cheap pictures on her walls of John Wesley, Charles Wesley, Jabez Bunting and other Methodist 'shining lights'. One day, on returning after a short absence, having left the door unlocked, she was shocked to find all these pictures with their faces turned to the wall and on the back of each, in chalk, the words 'Gone to Hell'.

So, maybe not such a tolerant community after all, although wherever you find religion, sex and politics, you will always find dissension and disagreement. We are indebted to Thomas Tonge for his wit, observation and memory. His recollections contain many more village names and many more unnamed daughters and, in Reg Worthington, we can say we managed to find a latter-day Thomas Tonge: both chroniclers of a village life that is as unique today as it was back then.

Walking around the village today, when the school is in and the wheelie bins are safely stowed away in the ginnels, and all you can hear is the occasional yelp of delight coming from the playground, you don't have to close your eyes to actually get a great sense of what it was like at the birth of the village.

It's there, before your very eyes. Esther's house, the shop, the school, the rippling cobbles, the small, neatly tended gardens, these days mostly laid to flowers and lawn. Then the view across the fields that would have slowly taken shape through the murk of a winter morning as the millworkers gathered their jackets and shawls around them, slowing to pass through the stile by the Apprentice House and allow the shivering children to join their ranks. You can imagine the cries of the infants, left behind by the single or widowed mothers, off to the mill. Left behind to be 'huddled' by the old crones or by a friend, also with child. The backward glance a man might have taken of his wife and babies, crowded in a cellar, awaiting his safe return and dreading it never happening. The fights, the rows, the laughs, the songs, the prayers, the sobs, the sighs, the sex, the deaths, the births. The village and all the life that teemed within it.

Strange then to contemplate that all this teeming life would pour over the tree-lined horizon, carrying their burdens, squabbles, hopes and fears, cramming itself into a building where life and death was settled in a more arbitrary manner and where they would spend the majority of their waking hours until their dying day. The mill itself.

CHAPTER TEN

Trouble and Strife

What delicious irony that, once enslaved to the mill, your very identity and immediate livelihood became inextricably linked with that of your workplace. If the mill failed, then so did you. Whatever threatened the bricks, mortar and metal was also your enemy. 'Beguiled' or simply fighting to survive? There were many threats, veiled and real, that washed up against the fortress walls of the mill in its long history, and there must have been many a child secretly wishing the walls would tumble and that they'd be transported back into the safety of their waiting families. If those families still existed.

The perennial threat to the security of the mill was of course the cotton trade itself, with its periodic fluctuations. There were many of these in the nineteenth century, for a variety of reasons, and many mills went under. The American Civil War of 1861–5 saw a huge drop in the availability of cotton, sparking what was appropriately known as the Cotton Famine. Quarry Bank wasn't immune. The mill memoranda show that this was felt most keenly in 1862, when production fell so much that the working week was reduced to three days.

Cotton prices rose, production stalled and the mill felt the beginnings of a depression.

You might think this would result in the wholesale laying-off of workers, but something more remarkable happened. Loans were made against future wages and small weekly stoppages arranged against the hoped-for return to better trading days. Fuel, mostly coal, was sold at a nominal price, and so were certain essential foodstuffs. Many men were found work in other parts of the Greg estate – the gardens, allotments and grounds. Again, was this pure altruism on the Gregs' part or were they ever conscious of how difficult it had been to attract and nurture a workforce in the first place and they weren't going to let them go without a fight? It does seem that everything that could be done, within financial reason, was put into practice to stave off the worst effects of the dire circumstances. Everything, that is, apart from supplying comparable working wages in the first place.

Wages at Quarry Bank were significantly lower than those in mills in, say, Manchester or Stockport. During the 1830s it was estimated that only 10 per cent of the workforce were earning more than 12s per week, while about 70 per cent were earning less than 9s per week. There were, however, mitigating circumstances. Quarry Bank attracted many agricultural labourers, unskilled in mill work and earning lower wages where they had worked before. 'Mr Muggeridge's Migrants', whom we met when they were leaving home, were examples of people who greatly increased their wages by working in the mill. What's more, the working conditions, while horrendous, did not hold a tallow candle to those suffered in the mills of Manchester and the like. Life expectancy in towns and cities for people doing this work was much lower than that at Quarry Bank. Few Manchester workers saw cushy retirement as the deserving James Henshall did, the ex-apprentice who became mill manager. And housing, as we have seen, was better at Styal. The village cottages were sound, if cramped, and the Apprentice House offered accommodation that was better than no house at all, or indeed, that experienced in the parish workhouses many had escaped from. So there's the balance: quality of life versus better wages.

Most millworkers never lived long enough to enjoy whatever they had earned over a short lifetime. Why not try and enjoy the relative security offered by Quarry Bank? Stay and raise a family, away from the filth and degradation offered up by the cities, safe in the knowledge that Quarry Bank was a kind of haven, free from the strife and lawlessness on their doorstep. Except, of course, it wasn't completely free from these influences. The outside world would make its presence felt.

Quarry Bank could not be completely insulated against the political movements of the early nineteenth century which brought great social upheaval. Even in this remote part of the country, word could spread, carried by those whose business took them further afield and those whose business brought them to the mill itself. Indeed, the Gregs encouraged travelling speakers to hold forth in the Methodist Chapel on many subjects which would have included travel, politics, religion and very probably suffrage. So what if most of the workers couldn't read, they could always listen to the talk of a changing world, and the talk was not always what they would have wanted to hear. After the end of the Napoleonic wars, in 1815, the country suffered massive unemployment and severe food shortages, fuelling civic unrest and a resentment at lack of voting rights. The working man grew angry at the lack of parliamentary representation – Manchester was completely unrepresented – and wanted a fair day's pay for a fair day's work. This, of course, affected thousands in the cotton industry, some of whom would have liked to have been paid at all. Radicalism spread and the flames of unrest were fanned by many eloquent, educated men such as John Doherty and Henry Hunt. The rich, powerful South feared the radical, poor North. Even those lucky or greedy enough to have become rich and powerful in the North feared the North. This culminated in a game-changing event: Peterloo, named both for its location near Manchester and the battle of Waterloo four years earlier.

This massacre still resonates today, symbolic of the common man fighting for rights against the elite. Here on hot, dusty St Peter's Field some eight miles from Quarry Bank in August 1819, a peaceful assembly of 60,000 protesters was charged by the mounted cavalry of the local Yeomanry, some sodden and inebriated by the ale they'd downed to help gird their loins against the unprotected women, men and children before them. They were swiftly joined by charging hussars and men of the Cheshire cavalry, trampling through the crowd, slashing at anyone in their way to apprehend the orator on the platform that day, Henry Hunt. Up to twenty men and women were killed in a matter of minutes, and many hundreds injured, most cut down by sabres. One woman, Mary Fildes, had slipped off the platform where she was delivering the flag of her women's movement and caught her dress on a nail. As she hung there, desperate for rescue, the Yeomen slashed at her with their sabres. Their bloodlust had become all the fiercer because she was a woman and, in staging such a display of solidarity with the working men, she was an affront to the honour and status of the Yeomen. Mary survived but many didn't, and they became an emblem for the stand women took that day: equal in death, equal in life.

This time Quarry Bank was not directly involved. But Samuel Greg and his son Robert Hyde were present at Peterloo and what they saw must have been relayed back to Quarry Bank by the end of that terrible day. If they were there, then it's not stretching credulity to suppose that some of their workforce could be there too. Or, at the very least, people known to them in Wilmslow. News would have spread fast: see how you're treated when you step out of line? Women, just like men, sliced down where they stood. Simply for wanting their basic human rights. Those predisposed to mutiny would have felt like gathering arms, those already cowed would have kept their collective heads down, not me, no chance! Just as Peterloo sent shockwaves through the whole of English society, it would have reverberated through the comparative calm of Styal. Keep out of it and you'll be all right. Want to know and feel what it's like in the city, in Manchester? There's your answer.

It was said that the lack of a coherent male rely to Peterloo, set back the attainment of votes for all men by fifty years. Paradoxically, the women's movement gained a respect and power it could never have dreamed of had not so many innocent women lost their lives and been injured. Whether the women and girls of Quarry Bank liked it or not, power was on its way. Hannah's eldest daughter, Elizabeth, exemplified the fact, going on to help found a public bathhouse in Liverpool with the help of an ex-apprentice girl, Kitty Wilkinson. Elizabeth would have been in the village and the Apprentice House, helping with the medicines and the education; she was a woman with an opinion, like her mother, and would have made herself heard. The apprentice girls must have listened to her, wide-eyed and agog.

More than twenty years after Peterloo, the outside world didn't just knock at Quarry Bank's door. It came crashing in.

For the only time in the whole of its history, the mill came under direct attack, by the so-called Plug Riots of 1842. The second series of *The Mill* deals with these riots, placing John Howlett, Daniel Bate and Esther Price at the heart of this version of events, but not necessarily on the same side. In 1842 Esther was twenty-two years old and waiting for William Whittaker's parents to die. John Howlett was forty-five and, with most of his family at work in the mill, their jobs were at risk. The real Daniel Bate was probably dead. Certainly, Howlett would have been sworn in as a special constable, and probably would have been proud to have done so. I feel sure the fiction of the television series captures the confusion most must have felt. If the real Esther was brave enough to run away and prove her age, manning the picket line would have been grist to her mill, she'd have relished it. But of course, in nineteenth-century reality, this was a man's job.

The Plug Riots had their roots very firmly planted in the same soil as Peterloo. On 4 May 1842, one Thomas Duncombe presented a petition to Parliament demanding six points set out as part of a Charter, detailing demands for better conditions and pay for Britain's industrial workers. It contained 3,250,000 signatures and the document's authors, who became known as the Chartists, must have been hopeful of a positive response. They had even included an attack on the monarchy, citing Queen Victoria's income of £164 17s 10d a day as compared with the daily wage of 'the producing millions'. It wasn't received well, being rejected by 287 votes to 47. There followed the 'long hot summer' of 1842 which was distinguished by an increasing number of strikes and retaliation by millowners. As with Peterloo, back in 1819, local land- and millowners became threatened and fearful. The Duke of Wellington advised Sir Robert Peel, the Prime Minister, to act decisively and send in the military, as had happened at Peterloo. He did and once again local Yeomanry and Hussars gathered around the streets of Manchester and the surrounding mill areas: Stalybridge, Dukinfield, Mossley, Glossop and Stockport.

Meanwhile, large groups of working people were encouraged to gather and hear prominent Chartist speakers. In the television series Daniel, Esther and John Doherty attend such meetings and are carried along with the righteous fervour of those protesting against the treatment of working folk in the mills. Their rallying cry was once again, 'a fair day's wage for a fair day's work'. The more the millowners resisted, the more they were spoken out against at the seemingly inflammatory meetings. A war of words threatened to spill over into outright war. Some millowners, hearing of attacks on other mills, do what they can to protect their own properties. Some, as with the Gregs, swear in their own special constables, exactly the kind of role taken up with some relish by John Howlett in the fictional version of the story. The heat of the summer boils over and mobs spill all over the North West, crashing through the meagre defences of the mills and literally removing the plugs from the boilers fuelling the mills' power. Thus creating the saying 'pulling the plug' and giving a name to the riots of that time. On 11 August, a large mob gathered in Stockport and then splintered off into factions, seeking out mills to attack and disable. Some took off in the direction of Styal.

In Wilmslow, a half company of the 60th Rifles was assembled for protection. At Quarry Bank, according to the mill memoranda, 'All able bodied men were sworn in as special constables', patrolling the neighbourhood night and day. What happened next is recorded sparsely. The mob arrived, spilling down the apprentices' cobbled path, and were met with some resistance. Evidently some of the millworkers were there and mingled with the visiting rebels, probably somewhere near the courtyard between the spinning and weaving buildings. Ironically for folk rioting to help put food on their tables, this area now holds the entrance to the restaurant. They weren't alone. Robert Hyde Greg was there in person, appealing for calm. Allegedly he quieted the crowd, claiming that the complaints and protests of the mob were largely down to the 'loose morals of working classes tippling in pot houses'. How exactly this subdued the riotous nature of the incomers is unclear, but the mill itself remained unscathed as the rioting crowd dispersed, but not before taking out their anger in other areas of Styal. The village shop was reported to have been 'gutted' and the women and girls in the crowd also 'gutted' the Apprentice House.

The Plug Riots were part of a movement that would help to stir up the General Strike of 1848, which, in turn, brought about real change for the working classes, yet Quarry Bank seemed immune, indifferent almost. Maybe Greg had indeed beguiled his slaves to such a degree that they feared the rebellious outside world as much as their masters did? Quarry Bank remained closed down for three weeks while the riots raged elsewhere that summer.

There is only one other instance of the mill being shut for any appreciable length of time and, when you consider the nature of the cause, you wonder why it didn't happen more often. The River Bollin was, and still is, the life source of Quarry Bank. Mostly it was harnessed by the quite brilliant engineering involved in damming and controlling its power. The Bollin was fed into the mill pond to the north of the mill. This was more of a lake, the very same lake that would one day claim the life of the lovesick John Knight. This in turn fed the head race, a flow of water that literally raced through the mill grounds, at one point dropping eighteen feet to help gain momentum. The ensuing torrent crashed through the huge buckets of the massive water wheel and drove the many gears and pulleys needed to power up the mill machines. Once spent, the water sped off via the tail race, spewing out back into the river, downstream at a place called the Giant's Castle. Both the head and the tail race are tunnels, blasted and hewn from the very rock the mill itself stands on. This way, via a series of sluices and gates, the Bollin was tamed. Until the day the river roared and shook off these man-made shackles.

As I write these words, in early 2014, we are reminded of the awesome power of nature, unleashed. Farmlands flooded, rivers raging, sea walls breached: the unstoppable force that is water. In 1872 there was what was documented as a 'terrible thunderstorm and a deluge of rain on the Macclesfield hills'. Normally all that was washed down from Macclesfield was the dye and waste from its mills, one actually owned by the Gregs themselves. This time was different and it happened without warning. A torrent raged down the valley, destroying all the dams built along its course. It took the top six feet off the weir as it hurtled towards the mill itself and carried away the 'saw pit' building, bundling it off downstream. The stone bridge separating the mill from the Greg gardens, which normally allows strolling visitors to gaze down at the river from some twelve to fifteen feet, was overwhelmed. On its way through the county, the torrent demolished five of its bridges. The whole of the valley was underwater and the river 'stood six feet deep in the Blowing room'. Some machinery and quantities of cotton and finished cloth were ruined. The mill shut down for a number of weeks, but, amazingly, no lives were lost. It must have been terrifying to stand helpless as the water began to power its way over the crumbling weir and flood on to the meadow outside the mill windows. There would have been frantic attempts to shut everything down without killing it all instantly and running the risk of uprooting the water wheel, possibly sending it crashing through the mill's foundations, skittling the bricks. It must have been a sobering sight, but the waters abated, the flooded rooms were cleaned, the machines were resurrected and the workers returned. Soon the walls were shaking anew and the mill was once again sucking the life from the river. It had all survived.

Beset by market forces, civil unrest, the power of the elements . . . there was another threat to the mill that may have brought in the outside world. Or not. It involved the actual money owed to the workers: the wages' heist of 1854. The greatest crime committed at Quarry Bank provides us with what is also the greatest mystery, and there doesn't appear to have been an apprentice child in sight. Sometime in the small hours between 15 and 16 December 1854, a storm blew up, howling through the skeletal arms of the denuded beeches and oaks and spewing forth torrents of rain. Incredibly, the whole of the mill was watched over by one man only. He was responsible for all the security for the whole site, and if he'd had any sense, he'd have been watching the fury of the weather unfold from behind closed but rattling window panes. Pushing sixty years of age, George Ollier wasn't a young man any more and his character, it seemed, was not conducive to being alone at night. He loved company. The 'Recollections of Thomas Tonge' pin him down, 'He was a character, spoke in the dialect of the "wiches" of which district he was a native and was a great spinner of wonderful yarns.' Instantly, a roll call of those great Dickensian characters appears in your mind: Magwitch, Bumble . . . and you can picture Old Olly, settling into his seat, pipe in hand, legs apart, shuffling to get comfortable and readying himself to tell stories to anyone who'd listen, particularly the young impressionable apprentices. Well, after that night he'd have another 'wonderful yarn' to spin. Yet strangely, he seems to have remained modestly tight-lipped about what happened, for there are no records of his testimony and, as far as the authorities would have been concerned, facts were thin on the ground.

George lived at No 7 Oak Cottages in Styal with a large family, so large in fact that some seemed to have spilled over into the cellars of No 8 where, along with John Howlett, George appears as joint head of the house. The 1851 census gives us the scale of the family. George, then aged fifty-five, occupation, watchman. Mary Ann, aged forty-five, so ten years younger than George. Lydia, twenty-five, occupation, carder, and with another word describing her situation: Widow. Susanna, twenty-four, occupation, throstler, unmarried. Sarah, age unknown, occupation, power loom weaver. Mary Ann, aged fourteen, occupation, throstler. Ann, aged twelve, occupation, winder. Eliza, aged ten and George, aged five, both scholars. The Ollier family had another member, though, George's spinster sister, 'Old Betty Ollier'. Thomas Tonge remembers her, 'a familiar figure, with her bedgown, striped petticoat, old fashioned bonnet and occasional half-length clay pipe – a very useful woman, especially at white washing'. So George had a large family to support, despite the small wages being brought in by some of his children. A widowed daughter, a spinster sister who did the odd bout of washing for folk. George's wages for this period are stated as 14 shillings per week, which wasn't that bad, but certainly wouldn't have had the family living in clover.

So, with a large family to provide for and his sixtieth birthday looming, on a dark and stormy night in December, George, being a storyteller, might well have been contemplating his fate and what kind of hand life had dealt him. Whether or not George kept himself dry and comparatively warm in the offices next to the mill manager's house is not known. What was known, and widely at that, was that all the paid hands queued at the window to the wages office every Friday, to receive their little cups of coins. A smaller number of people would also have known that this office contained the only safe in the mill. Those not in the know, and with time on their hands to speculate, could also have worked this out. Someone, piecing it all together, could also have realised that, in order for the millhands to be paid at all on a Friday, the money would have had to be transported from the bank either on the Thursday before, or on the morning of the Friday itself. Had that someone been in a position to see the wages being brought in to the mill on a regular basis? Was someone in the wages office itself keeping tabs on it all? Whatever the circumstances and whoever was involved, sitting behind a seemingly impenetrable safe door, and, bricked into the office wall itself, was the best part of £300. The entire amount due to be paid the following afternoon, after clocking-off time. In contemporary terms, this was almost £14,000 worth of coinage.

Sitting in the steeply rising valley, Quarry Bank Mill has one road in and that same road out. The cobbled driveway that takes all visitors, grand or poor, honest or villainous, past the Apprentice House and away to Wilmslow. The mill, on the other side from the road, looks out over the Bollin and across the meadow, to the other steep valley wall, with only the one small path leading through the private Greg gardens and into the North Woods. Anyone contemplating the removal of £300 worth of pennies and sixpences must have calculated the weight involved. They would have needed sacks. They would have needed a cart, and therefore a horse. They would have needed heavy tools to even attempt to break into that safe. They would have needed a decent working knowledge of the office layout, the position of the safe. Most of all they would have needed to feel secure that they would not be disturbed. They needed the cover of darkness and they would have needed a clear run at the job. They would have needed old George Ollier out of the way.

So, as the storm raged on, and as he peered through the driving rain, George was getting close to making the biggest decision of his life, his defining moment. At what stage should he, as the night watchman, decide that the level and state of the Bollin was becoming a threat to the mill itself? George would have realised the possible terrible consequences of a flood and further realised that if it happened on his watch, then it would be a personal as well as a business disaster. Being the nightwatchman was a steady job. Sure, the wage wasn't handsome, but at nearly sixty, what other jobs could he expect to do? He would risk everything, his home at Oak Cottages, his family's welfare, his children's future. All would suffer if he didn't act decisively. At some point George lurched into action and left the warmth of wherever he'd been holed up to pitch himself out into the fury of the storm. The sluice gates, determining how much water was allowed to access the head race, would need to be turned against the rapidly rising river. George would have assessed the state of them and made the second most important decision of his life. He needed help. He had two options. The mill manager's house stood a few feet away, he could raise the manager and the pair of them could attempt to turn the gates. Or he could make haste, as fast as his fifty-nine-year-old legs could carry him, to the village at Styal to get more help. The only way to the village was back up the cobbled road, a sharp left just before the Apprentice House, and then across the open fields for another five minutes or so. Did it cross his mind to knock up some of the larger lads in the Apprentice House, or even the steward himself? If it did, he resisted and ploughed on through the wind and rain into Styal. Perhaps he had it in mind to pummel on the doors of an engineer or two for the task, someone with specialist knowledge?

Whatever thoughts raced through his head, from the second he strode on up that road, passing Quarry Bank House (where his very master lay asleep) and disappeared from sight, any would-be robbers would have seized this seemingly golden opportunity and hastened to the office door. Of course they would have had to be convinced that George would not return for some time. Surely, short of summoning the very flood themselves, they could not have known where George was going, or indeed, when he would return and with how many other men. They either took a huge risk or they had enough men to hand to confront any people getting in their way. Perhaps they had enough inside information to know that they would not be interrupted while they carried out the robbery? It all hinged on the actions of that rotund old man.

George would have arrived, breathlessly, in Styal, some ten or so minutes after leaving. Let's say he paused to regain his breath, having crested the valley's steep incline. Fifteen minutes at the most. Another five to raise sufficient help – this was, after all, an emergency. A further ten minutes back downhill and with the wind at their backs? Thirty minutes, a long time when the river was swelling at the gates, testing the hinges, beating on the panels. So our intrepid thieves had around half an hour. First they had to break in through the correct office door. Then another interior door, providing it hadn't been left open by George. Maybe the thieves were pleasantly surprised to find all their initial obstacles removed? Maybe George, in his haste to save the mill, had simply fled without locking a single door? Benefits to both watchman and thieves, precious minutes saved. Next, the main obstacle. The safe.

There was no easy or quiet way to hack through the thick metal door and the thieves would have been grateful for the howling of the storm for a reason other than that it had taken George out of the picture; it covered their noise. Having ransacked the safe and bagged the huge amounts of coins, they'd have struggled out and loaded the waiting cart. Then they would have had to race away, back up the same road that George and his men would surely have been using to run back down to the sluice gates. It's possible they were literally, mob-handed and that they sped off across the meadow, or up through the South Woods along the river bank, carrying the many heavily laden bags. The more men involved the smaller the shares. The more men involved the greater the chance of someone talking and getting caught. Either way, the greatest risk of all was turning up in the first place and not expecting to meet anyone in their way. But they did this and got away with every last penny of their £295 haul.

How surprised would George have been to discover the shattered safe? Was he surprised at all? Did he curse his luck that, in leaving his post to 'save' the mill from flood, he left it wide open to theft? Was he censured for his action, or applauded? Did he lose his job? No. George was still there at Oak Cottages in the 1861 census and still noted as a watchman, aged sixty-two, although by then he'd moved to No 8.

A reward was posted offering £50 to anyone with information on the theft. Presumably George was questioned thoroughly, accounting for his every movement. Presumably he had witnesses for his return to the sluice gates. No single piece of evidence ever came to light and no one ever volunteered a single scrap of information. If ever a weather eye was kept out for the 1850s version of the new Porsche in the drive, then it was never reported. Whoever had planned and executed the robbery had done so meticulously and perfectly. For they were never caught.

On 7 October 1866, George Ollier was buried in Wilmslow, aged sixty-seven and leaving widow Mary Ann behind, for her to pass away two years later. George's, some would say, brave and dramatic role on that textbook stormy night, and the ensuing scandal makes for a great story. Yet nothing survives of that night, other than the bare facts. An audacious robbery took place while the watchman was away, saving the mill. End of story.

So, how did the mill survive this particular assault on its business? One story goes that Robert Hyde Greg stood the workers' wages himself until the moneys could be transferred once more from the bank. I wonder if the workers toasted their master and saviour that night in the Ship Inn? And if they did, I wonder who had enough in their pockets to stand the first round? One thing was certain: the mill survived, the workers never felt a thing. Another potential wave of threat had crashed uselessly against the fortress and ebbed away, leaving only a story in its wake. A unique story however, one of many in the remarkable tapestry of this unique place and its unique people. The involvement of Robert Hyde, saving the day, also points up the contradictory nature of the Gregs. Philanthropy versus mill owning, surely you can't do justice to both at the same time?

Without the Greg family there is no Quarry Bank, there is no village, and people who spent their whole lives there would have been scattered to the wind. The sweat, ingenuity and hard graft of the masters permeates the bricks of Quarry Bank just as much as that of the workforce, and their assiduous collating of the archive material means that we are even able to look into their past in such a detailed and rich manner. You cannot stand before the mill and not wonder what made them who they were.

CHAPTER ELEVEN

The Masters

When Samuel Greg stood in the meadow, over two centuries ago, and gazed across the Bollin and began to dream of his mill and his dynasty, did he imagine it still standing when men had stood on the Moon and landed robots on Mars? He may not even have imagined it beyond the arrival of the train. But build it he did, one brick at a time, one life at a time. And then, with Hannah at his side and with ambitious sons waiting impatiently in the wings, they shaped an extraordinary future for their families and the folk who would work for them. Everyone at Quarry Bank, inextricably linked, for better, for worse, for richer for poorer – married for life. It is impossible to understand how things were at Quarry Bank without understanding the Gregs, in all their contradictory glory.

We've had a glimpse of Samuel's father, Thomas Greg of Belfast, the successful merchant who had immigrated to Ireland from his native Scotland. He had businesses in England, Russia and New York, and connections to the slave trade that continued right up to its abolition. He was also a friend and patron of Lord Hillsborough, and indeed named an estate after him as part of his West Indies properties in Dominica. Thomas didn't manage all this on his own, however. He had a formidable ally in his business partner, Waddell Cunningham. Together they ran their several businesses in their own distinctive way. Thomas remained with his growing family in Belfast while the colourful Waddell was the troubleshooter, almost literally. He thought nothing of riding through the streets of New York in an open cart, seeking out men he reckoned had crossed him in business. Once he found them, he would leap down and beat them up. This ruthlessness helped forge a successful empire, built partly on the bones of African slaves and bolstered by Celtic grit via the shameless trade of smuggling and piracy under the banner of 'privateering'.

By 1776, times were uncertain, his business fortunes fluctuating wildly. That's when Thomas sent away his two oldest sons, Samuel and Thomas Jnr, to seek their own fortunes, keeping his youngest son, Cunningham (no doubt named after the wild Waddell), at home. Samuel was only eight, Thomas sixteen. They were to lodge with their mother's brothers, Robert and Nathaniel Hyde of Denton, Manchester, and learn the textile trade. Thomas didn't stick around and young Samuel Greg found that his Uncle Nathaniel seemed to harbour a certain jealousy towards him. Nathaniel and his wife had managed to produce seven daughters but, to that date, no sons, who would be heirs to the business. It's likely that Nathaniel saw the young Samuel as a cuckoo in his well-feathered nest. This certainly wouldn't apply to Thomas Jnr, who turned his back on the textile trade, leaving brother Samuel to his fate at the hands of the uncles. Thomas Jnr claimed he owed nothing to his family but 'an indifferent education', which might seem a tad harsh, but Thomas clearly knew his own mind and went on to make a fortune in marine insurance. He became known as 'Thomas of Coles', and his country residence at Coles, Hertfordshire, was reputedly a place where he entertained in a grand manner, becoming a venue known for its many 'high jinks'. You could say that, as far as Nathaniel was concerned, Thomas Jnr's removal of himself from the picture meant that he only had Samuel to contend with.

Nathaniel was eighteen years younger than his brother Robert, and prone to prolonged bouts of drunkenness and gambling, a heady cocktail. This wilful unreliability must have prompted the older Robert to realise that their business would not be overly secure with Nathaniel at the helm. For as much as Nathaniel persecuted Samuel, the childless Robert favoured him. Nathaniel thought it a good idea to secure a parish and a future as a member of the clergy for young Samuel. To avoid this fate, and get Samuel away from Nathaniel's jealous wrath, Robert sent him to school. First in Harrow, then York, where he studied under the renowned Greek scholar and reputed flogger, Dr Parr. We learn from Michael Janes's invaluable book *From Smuggling to Cotton Kings* that Samuel would complain he was regularly flogged '*before* school', deeming this 'an improper use of authority'. It's possible that this early introduction to corporal punishment and, in his eyes, its unjust application, made Samuel carefully consider its use in his mills. Such punishment could force victims in different directions. They become inured to the violence and therefore inured to its effects, being more likely to use it; or they grow to oppose it.

It was while in York that Samuel began to display characteristics that would surface in his later years, those with Hannah. Allegedly Samuel used to 'shoot billet-doux' through the windows of girls who lived across the street from his lodgings. He was clearly attracted to the girls he saw there, but chose an anonymous approach, seemingly baulking at actually meeting any of them. He was also reprimanded by his dancing master for squeezing his partner's hands too firmly. Surely this was a sign of a young man who was somewhat embarrassed and clumsy in the company of the opposite sex? Someone for whom successfully attending to affairs of the heart didn't come easily? There are many instances in later life where Samuel is described as a charming man, but I do get the feeling he was more comfortable in the company of men.

On his return, Samuel proved himself a useful acquisition to the Hyde textile trade, even being sent abroad to further his understanding in the industry, and when Robert Hyde died in 1782, he left his building and all the goods to Samuel, so sure was Robert that Samuel would succeed. Nathaniel recognised the writing on the wall and reluctantly agreed he would also leave all business affairs to Samuel on his death, with the likely proviso that he, Nathaniel, never managed a son. As we have already seen, fate stepped in at this point and greatly favoured Samuel. With Nathaniel's son making an appearance only after his father's death, Samuel got the lot. In a few years' time, he was to have even more. He'd built his mill, was well on with the other mills dotted around Manchester and was establishing an excellent reputation for quality goods. He'd even managed to find a perfect partner for life in the wilful Hannah.

As we've seen, Hannah and Samuel had a mixed start to their romantic life. Once installed in Samuel's house at King Street, Manchester, we know from her letters that Hannah felt out of her depth domestically, and overburdened by his family and his coarse fellow merchants. How she longed for the kind of home she'd probably dreamed of back in Liverpool. She desperately missed her friends too. In particular, Hannah Mary Rathbone, wife of her good friend William Rathbone. Hannah had sought Mrs Rathbone's advice on many subjects, feeling she could speak or write freely. In his book *A Lady of Cotton*, author David Sekers offers this insight into their relationship: 'For forty years Hannah Mary was a constant and intimate friend of Hannah, a person to whom Hannah could pour out her hopes and her fears, discuss the nursing of children, their illnesses and their death. It was a relationship in which emotions were not concealed.' Unlike her marriage, then. The passage continues: 'Hannah Mary Rathbone's at Greenbank at Toxteth Park represented a model to which Hannah probably aspired. It was an elegant base in which to entertain scientific, literary and political visitors from afar, as well as Liverpool reformers, while at the same time offering a rural haven for the children.'

Samuel's bachelor pad at King Street could not be further from this ideal. Manchester was scruffy, dirty and dangerous. Hannah wrote furiously to her sister, telling her that Mr Greg actually allowed dogs into the house! Sister Elizabeth wrote back with sisterly affection, but also with the wisdom of a wife. Her advice for new wives? 'Not to contradict their husbands the first twelvemonth', adding helpfully that, 'whilst she has married a man aware of her intellectual endowments, men are still the superior sex'. Things were bad enough indoors, surely there wasn't anything the outside world could do to make them worse?

Samuel had been born into a family belonging to the collection of Rational Dissenters, a more radical and intellectual wing of the Presbyterian folk to be found in Ireland. Once ensconced at King Street, one thing liberal Hannah did manage was to get her socially reluctant husband to join the Manchester Literary and Philosophical Society, just after their marriage in 1790. Was this an indulgence to keep his new wife happy? Very probably. Both of them being of dissenting and reforming mind, Samuel the less enthusiastic of the two, there was at least common ground. But this in itself brought particular problems. Manchester reformists quickly took up a sympathetic stance with the poor people of France when the French Revolution began in 1789. Hannah and Samuel expressed their sympathies too, but when that revolution spawned widespread atrocities and began to pall in the eyes of the onlooking world, most of the reformist community in Manchester were just as quick to distance themselves from it. Hannah and Samuel were less speedy to speak against the revolution, and they and Dissenters in general began to be ostracised by Manchester society. When the French Revolution turned sour, suspicious fingers began to be pointed, malicious whispers could be heard in the trading corridors in the city as the landowners and merchants joined ranks and started to shuffle their corporate backs against the walls.

The family's Irish connection were not helping matters. Inspired by the revolutions in France and America, radical elements in Irish society were protesting vociferously against British rule, demanding reform and autonomy. The Loyalist government would not give an inch, mobilising the military to hunt down Republican sympathisers. Samuel's younger brother Cunningham Greg must have given the authorities some ground for suspicion. In 1797 his house was attacked by soldiers, some allegedly tossing a Greg family portrait out of a window. Cunningham survived the experience – like his namesake Waddell, he'd show a talent for self-preservation. If Cunningham was to present Samuel and Hannah with one headache, Samuel's sister, Jane, was something else all together.

The author David Sekers tells us that Jane was already known as an outspoken friend of many leading British and Irish radicals. It was said that she 'used her charms and connections secretly to convey messages vital to the United Irishman's cause'. Jane was a renowned letter-writer and seemingly had little or no compunction in using these letters for this purpose. Some were intercepted. In May 1797, the Belfast Postmaster reported her activities. Things were getting too hot for her, and when tensions exploded in the Irish Rebellion of 1798, she was shipped over to Manchester to stay with Samuel and Hannah. They realised they were about, more or less, to start harbouring a spy, and Hannah feared the worst. She was worried for Samuel, that Jane's letters might 'bring suspicion upon him'. She remarked that at times she could not sleep at night for fear of the knock at the door. So, what little common ground Hannah did find with Samuel in these early years ironically brought little comfort. Sister Jane herself clearly did feel comfortable residing with her brother and his wife, for she seems to have remained with them for the rest of her life, and indeed, beyond. Jane died in 1817 and is buried with Samuel and Hannah in the family vault at Wilmslow Parish Church.

Meanwhile, Hannah must have feared that her married life was doomed. The terror of the Irish situation was not helped by the very real fear of the wars in Europe and with Napoleon. She so dreaded domiciliary visits that according to her daughter Ellen, 'Invasion too was feared, and my mother kept all ready for flight along with her children.' Hannah also often worried for Samuel when he left the house, simply because she felt he was the 'only Irish gentleman in town'. She certainly would not have wanted to rear her children in this poisonous atmosphere. In a letter to William Rathbone, written in the winter of 1805–6, Hannah relates visiting the house in King Street that they'd kept on, and the terrible experience of finding a destitute pauper woman on her doorstep: 'yesterday a poor woman fell in a fit on our steps and in less than two hours after I took her into the house expired almost in my arms – an affecting Circumstance before the eyes of my Children and Servants'.

Hannah often spoke of the 'dark ages' of her own childbearing years; the rearing of children and the domestic duties (entertaining drunken merchants from Yorkshire) as having 'brought me down from the skies'. Hannah also recalled that simply having serious thoughts and reflections was regarded in the household as being 'a flagrant violation of the Irish code'. In other words Samuel didn't much care for it. How these circumstances must have reminded her of her earlier, written yearning for a husband sensitive to her intellect and opinion. Someone more like herself. Now that Samuel had captured his prize, had he simply reverted to the kind of 'shallow' man she'd sought to escape when in Liverpool? A man who wasn't constant in his views? Hannah's misgivings would have had more ammunition in the scandalous matter of Samuel's brother Cunningham. And it was nothing to do with politics.

Dark deeds had come to light in Ireland. The seeds must have been sown when Cunningham had been left behind at home. As he grew up and watched his older brothers carve a future for themselves, he clearly felt he'd in some way been cheated. Maybe, like his illustrious, or notorious, namesake, he craved adventure, but lacked the gumption to go after it. He certainly didn't lack the guile. Cunningham developed the habit of teasing his many sisters by telling them, convincingly, that their grandfather was a blacksmith – the shame! Cunningham became a gambler and eventually persuaded his father, the elderly Thomas, to leave him everything when he died. Which he did, in 1796; all other family were disinherited.

It was rumoured that Cunningham also locked some poor old man up until, he too, surrendered his inheritance. He then did likewise to some old lady in her dotage, tricking her out of her money. None of this was proven, but his track record with his own father stood against him, the rumours persisted and the mud stuck.

Thomas Jnr, already rich and comfortable in his country seat at Coles, never spoke to Cunningham again, but Samuel kept in touch. Was this the softer, forgiving side to Samuel? Maybe he'd have felt differently if he'd not been doing so well himself, and needed the money? Whatever his reasons, Samuel clearly felt it was required of him as the only older brother still speaking to Cunningham to reel the miscreant in and give him what for. Cunningham was duly invited to the Greg home, where Samuel warned the ladies of the house that they should retire early after dinner so that Samuel could deliver to his wayward brother a 'wawful wigging'! The ladies dutifully did so, leaving the men alone and breathlessly awaiting the fearful result. If it hadn't involved a breach of decorum, you could almost imagine them crowded around a keyhole, shushing each other and straining for a whisper of sound. They would have been sorely disappointed when there was no slamming of doors and the raising of manly voices. After Cunningham had gone to bed they all asked Samuel what had happened. He told them he'd reprimanded Cunningham severely on the enormity of his conduct, which the black sheep had listened to quietly and respectfully. Then, when Samuel had said his piece, Cunningham had eventually replied, 'Well, Sam, if you had been in my place would not you have done the same?' A staggered Samuel caved in. He supposed he would!

This hardly reflects well on Samuel. All bark and no bite? Telling the ladies one thing, then behaving differently with the men? Or simply the act of a pragmatic man confronted with logic? Whichever, Cunningham was back in the fold and visited the Gregs many times thereafter.

Altogether, those early years in Manchester gave Hannah much cause for concern. David Sekers describes how 'the scales began to fall from her eyes, making her look at her husband in a new light'. When Samuel was returned from a cricket match, drunk and unable to stay on his horse, I can imagine he was probably at his happiest. A boozy day out with his friends, a bit of sport, not an intellectual argument in sight. Happy days. Not so for Hannah, who once more turned to her most regular confidante during these trying times, her diary: 'knowing nothing as to former habits & c . . . – tho' learning his character only from himself how impossible it seemed to me that I could be deceived. His kind sister laughed at my distress – for she knew better.' Hannah's letters to her family became more melancholy and the writing of them often brought her to tears. Once, Samuel came across a tearful Hannah, 'Mr G displeased at finding me in tears over a letter home. I assured him I only wanted his kindness and approbation to make me easy and happy and should have it if he would judge & feel for himself but not if thro others who did not know me enough.' Who were these 'others' and how had they displayed their erroneous opinions of Hannah?

There were the servants to start with. Hannah had fallen foul of Samuel's domestic staff, including insolent maids, sulky footmen and downright rude grooms. Hannah tells us via another letter home, 'Mr Greg's footman refused to go behind the coach – but was obliged by his master.' Refused? What on earth was going on? It got worse. 'The Groom refused to bring in Coal – and was dismissed. I wished the footman had met the same return for repeated insolence.' Was it simply that they did not like Hannah? Perhaps Samuel the appeaser had let them get away with a more relaxed way of servitude. They'd had it too easy and he hadn't been tough enough. This is at odds with Samuel the determined and crusading businessman, but, as we already suspect, Samuel could be a different man with different people. As if it wasn't bad enough to have to tackle uppity servants, Hannah also had to entertain string upon string of Samuel's circle, most of whom she'd never met. This took its strain. It was said that she was distant and uninvolved. Back to the diary: 'Wednesday: My cousin, Miss K and I sat up for company – very formal – and me not even knowing the names when we heard them – should have been much more embarrassed if Miss Kennedy had not been with us.'

You can almost picture the scene, as hugely pregnant pauses were filled only by the clatter of teacups being almost thrown at them by dissatisfied maids and disgruntled manservants. One guest, Mrs Hamilton, had the temerity to write to her mother, actually complaining about Hannah, saying, 'that I never called or seemed to care for Mr G's friends – a charge the most unjust that could have been found'. Mrs Hamilton did not stop there, saying to Hannah's face that, 'I think you have no joy with us for you are always wishing to be somewhere else.' Perhaps Mrs Hamilton had struck a chord with the miserable Hannah. Even visits by the renowned novelist Mrs Gaskell, who would probably have known the Gregs through her uncle Dr Holland, didn't bring Hannah the intellectual solace she might have expected. Elizabeth Gaskell was no supporter of the cotton trade or, seemingly, anyone involved in it. In her novel, *Cranford*, Gaskell describes Miss Betty Barker's fears that Mary Smith's father might have become involved in that 'horrid cotton trade,' and as having 'dragged his family down out of aristocratic society'. Elizabeth Gaskell's own opinions were not so far removed from her fictional characters'. Of a visit by Mrs Robert Greg and her sisters to Elizabeth's own cousin Bessy, she was to say, 'I don't care an atom for them, yet shall have to be tidy and civil.' She goes on to describe them as cousin Bessy's 'great cronies'.

What kind of family had Hannah fallen into? By now, she had given birth to eight of her thirteen children. Three of them died at birth. She was exhausted. She sought 'mental medicine'. She sought distraction. She was a desperate woman and something had to give. Just in time, enter Samuel the appeaser.

Samuel had often rented a farm at Oak's Fold, adjoining his rented lands at Quarry Bank. It was a place of recuperation and calm for Hannah, somewhere the children could run from their front door and not be confronted with filth and mortal danger. Here the oaks and pine trees were augmented by newly planted beeches in the heavily wooded valley. They created oases of cool respite during the hot summer months and shelter from the autumn winds, when they would shake like so many grand sails on a sea-going liner. Cannily, to enhance the rural idyll of Quarry Bank, Samuel had ordered those beeches to be planted on the steep slopes lining the valley. Not only did they look good but they had a practical purpose too. They helped form a canopy of tall trees that acted like an umbrella, containing all the moisture rising from the river and keeping the valley damp. On misty summer mornings the valley would cling to its mist, gathering the moist air around its tallest trees like a shroud. The sun, when it rose, would suck the steam out of the chill cobbles in the mill lane and make the lawns and meadows almost hiss with its heat. Perfect conditions for the manufacture of cotton, which sucked the very moisture from the air around it.

With the mill under full steam, Samuel ordered the building of what was to be Hannah's salvation: the Greg mansion at Quarry Bank. Here was Hannah's permanent rural retreat. A safe place for her rapidly growing family. A pleasant, elegant house where she could happily entertain all those politicians, artists, thinkers, writers and reformers. She gathered people around her like a comfort blanket, smothering them with her good graces, her impeccable manners and her much loved, glowing children. Samuel played the host, charming and accommodating, but it wasn't exactly to his liking. This was Samuel the appeaser again, indulging his adored wife, finally giving her what she wanted. It wasn't that Samuel was socially inept or uninterested, but I believe he was happier being socially active with his own kind. Indeed, on a visit to Ireland with Samuel, to get to know his large family better, Hannah noted, 'seeing Mr S G such a different Being to what he left home, he looks twenty years younger and in such delight from morning to night . . . and I am pleased to see Mr G proud of his own children even among those he has been accustomed to consider as Standards.'

How did Hannah see her life shaping up in her more mature years? Perhaps the best illustration of what she achieved was left by the great American nature artist, John James Audubon, visiting England for the first time to seek patrons for his books of illustrations of the birds of America. He'd already gleaned an extremely unflattering impression of Manchester, where he described the housing conditions as being worse than those of 'Louisiana negroes'. On the recommendation of the Rathbones, Hannah invited him to Quarry Bank in September 1826. Perhaps this would make a better impression. He had already attended a debate put on in the school rooms in Styal, one of many encouraged by Hannah and offered up to the village to attend. He had even dined with Samuel in Manchester, and when invited to meet with a Professor Smyth and then dine and stay at Quarry Bank House, he was not disappointed, 'One evening spent with him and the fair, kind circle at the Quarry Bank is worth a hundred such . . . as I had last evening.' Audubon remarked about Samuel that he, 'addresses his children in the most patriarchal style I ever heard and with a kindness only equaled by my friends at Green Bank'. He goes on to qualify Samuel's style: 'yet there is a bluntness in his speech at times'. How Hannah must have secretly winced. Audubon's next visit was his most rewarding, where he was shown a weaver's cottage and, noting the stuffed birds, was encouraged to shoot some himself, so that he could draw them better. His delight at this visit is a ringing endorsement for Hannah's achievement in making Quarry Bank House a place of refinement and family, for her the perfect companions.

> . . . from Green Bank to Quarry Bank, from one pleasure to another, not like the butterfly that skips from flower to flower & merely sees their beauties, but more I hope, as a bee, gathering honeyed knowledge. The next evening Mr Greg was in high spirits, so was his lady . . . Much entertaining poetry was read and repeated, we had a little music and a great deal of interesting conversation, much of it about his home country.

So Samuel delighted his guest and his wife, relaxed, talking about Ireland and with his family surrounding him. Audubon concludes memorably:

> Mrs Greg is one of those rare examples of the superior powers of thy sex over ours when education and circumstance are combined – She is most amiable, smart, quick, witty, positively learned, with an incomparable memory and as benevolent as Woman can be

– her and her husband form the finest picture of devoted, tender and faithful attachment I ever met with.

A far cry from being tongue-tied when faced with embittered, disobedient servants, and from falling off your horse, several pints the worse for wear.

The television series joins Hannah and Samuel in the twilight of their enduring marriage, just before Samuel's fictionally premature death. He, at the time of his death and, indeed, years before this, was a man marking time and getting in the way of progress. In dramatic terms, Hannah was the character with more potential, and so survives Samuel. What is true is that we see a couple at ease with each other and at ease with their achievements. Only then does the show go on to tackle the awfully thorny issue of the Greg involvement in the slave trade. Hannah came from a background of reformers and abolitionists. Samuel came from a background of slavers. They could not have been further apart in their appreciation of the issue, yet there is little discernible written evidence of arguments about this between the two. In the series, with Samuel gone, Hannah is confronted regarding her shame, first by John Doherty, then by the appearance of Peter, the ex-Dominican slave. This gives us a commendable insight into what must have been an internal conflict for Hannah, and helps resolve our feelings towards what her opinion must have been.

And all the time there was the mill itself, hunched over the Bollin like a huge asthmatic monolith, shuddering and booming with the effort of spitting out the cotton, as a constant reminder. Every time she threw open a window in summer, or pushed open a door to take a stroll through her beloved gardens, it was there. Did she mind? Probably, but there were few complaints. If anything the mill and its apprentices gave Hannah something she'd lacked all her adult life, even with the birth and rearing of her children. A purpose.

Hannah found the liberal and intellectual need she felt was missing from her life was supplied by the education of her own children and the care of the working children: 'I am persuaded that love is my forte and genius.' However, where the Greg children were concerned, she and Samuel were not in perfect accord. Hannah wanted fully rounded gentlemen as sons and always exhorted them to a 'higher level' of learning and sophistication. To further this end she sent her sons on excursions abroad (it was on one of those trips that Robert Hyde struggled with which sister to bestow his affections on). For his part, Samuel wasn't so sure. His opinion on education was that it was all fine and good, but wasted unless put to some practical application. Many of their sons went on to be farmers and harboured desires to be artists or writers. Samuel must have spun in his grave as if attached to his very own waterwheel. Whatever he felt, Hannah got her own way – again.

She felt it was her duty to extend this love and care to the education of the apprentice children, setting up the school room in the Apprentice House and later the separate school for the children of the village. The illustrious Dr Holland supplied medical care for the children's bodies, while Hannah's pastoral care took in their spiritual education, fired by her Unitarian beliefs. As far as the child apprentices were concerned, Hannah did her level best to get her hands metaphorically dirty. Over and above this, such was her immersion in all things cotton that Samuel paid her the greatest of compliments in his armoury. When he was away on business, he felt able to stay away more frequently because he trusted her to 'look after things'. Hannah found this a great compliment and 'honour'. She'd come a long way.

Hannah's eldest daughter, Elizabeth, was herself was a fascinating character, given, in her youth, to having 'flights of fancy'. In one of her letters resting in the archives she documents a fantasy she had, imagining herself a slave girl in the West Indies ordered to kill William Rathbone (who she later married) and being tortured for not doing so! She is then rescued by Richard Rathbone under the secret name of 'Mr Mollineux'. This evidently romantic girl was clearly encouraged in her aspirations by her mother, and also borrowed heavily from her father's family's slaving past. Perhaps she had shown a keen interest in Uncle Cunningham and the Irish connection with Dominica. The Greg family provided plenty of material.

We also need to consider the Greg family members following Samuel and Hannah into the cotton trade. Of their five sons, the eldest, Thomas Tylston, did not enter the cotton trade at all, having been named by Samuel's older brother Thomas of Coles as his heir. Robert Hyde was second in line. In many ways, he was the perfect inheritor of Quarry Bank. He modernised when it was necessary and secured the mill's immediate future. He did not renege on the treatment of his apprentice workers, although by then there were some laws offering them protection anyway. In fact, it could be said that of all of Samuel's sons, despite their differences, Robert Hyde was the best suited to business and understood his responsibilities well. The first thing he did was to ship in the weaving looms, the second to build a mansion in Styal, Norcliffe Hall, befitting the role of a millowner.

The next son was John Greg, who took over the mills in Lancaster and Caton. Samuel Jnr helped out at Quarry Bank, learning his trade alongside Robert Hyde. He was clearly impressed with the way Quarry Bank was run as he adopted a similar style when he took over at Bollington. Finally William Rathbone Greg, the youngest brother, took over the Bury Mill.

Whatever hopes Samuel Snr may have harboured for his sons, Samuel Jnr and William did not come up to scratch. Of William, it was said that he was 'too sanguine in practical matters . . . not having the faculty of sustained attention which is the pith and marrow of success in such as business as this'. In a letter from William to his sister Elizabeth Rathbone, he tellingly reveals, 'I wonder how long philosophy or indecision will induce me to continue the dog's life I am leading here, I never open a book . . . rise at 5.30 am and go to bed at 10 pm and toil like a galley slave all day . . .' An interesting use of metaphor for someone reaping the benefits of his grandfather's past connections.

Samuel Jnr fared no better. In fact it could be said that he fared the worst. He had the notion that Bollington would not only ape the altruistic model of his father's mill at Quarry Bank, but exceed it. Samuel Jnr supplied not only health care, but insisted on treating his workers almost as equals. He wanted to create a Utopian community, and didn't overly concern himself with the dirty business of profit and loss. His lofty aspirations came crashing down around his ears in an alarming manner. In one of his actual attempts to improve the production of goods in the mill, he tried to introduce new, specialist stretching machinery to the workforce. They didn't like it and went out on strike. Samuel couldn't believe he was being betrayed in this way, after all he'd done for his workers, whom he come to think of as almost friends. Samuel suffered some kind of breakdown, removing himself from everyday life and refusing to speak to any worker ever again. He cut a solitary and saddened figure, stalking alone through the town of Bollington, on the rare occasions he was actually seen in public.

Were William and Samuel over-educated by Hannah, against Samuel Snr's better judgement? Were their moral and intellectual expectations always going to be thwarted by a life in the mills? Certainly Samuel Snr had foreseen this turn of events when cautioning that any good education was wasted unless put to some practical application. To be fair to William Rathbone, he did put his shoulder to the wheel in helping to rescue Bollington along with Robert Hyde. Together they pulled it back from the brink of financial ruin between 1847 and 1850, even though William had to let his own mill in

Bury suffer as a result. No sooner was Bollington back in profit than older brother John declared that he'd always fancied it for himself. William was outraged. Nonetheless in 1850 John took over at Bollington and the Bury mill was sold off. William had seen enough and retired from the cotton trade, becoming a prolific writer of pamphlets and articles, later joining Her Majesty's Stationery Office. We can only hope he was happier there, no longer sweating away like a 'galley slave'.

Robert Hyde was described by those who knew him as a 'very reserved person'. He could apparently appear 'remote, stern and meticulous'. He, like his father Samuel, did not sail through his courtship with his future wife unscathed. Robert Hyde wrote to his future wife, Mary, during their courtship, mentioning the 'fatal ring' that he was now sending back to her. Evidently Mary must have declined it first time around, for whatever reasons. Perhaps she accepted his proposal initially, then they had a falling out and she gave him the ring back? Either way, they had obviously worked through their problems and the ring was being returned by Robert Hyde. He declared that the ring was now 'fatal to only my anxieties . . . My happiness through life must now depend on your affections, therefore cherich [sic] it and preserve it for me as you would a charm on which my existence depended.' It doesn't say much for his romantic persuasion that he appears to be returning the ring in a letter.

In another similarity with his father, Robert Hyde also had trouble with a son. In Robert's case, it was his firstborn, Robert Philips, and the feeling of antipathy seemed to have been mutual. Mary called their eldest 'Bobbums', spoiling him rotten, which must have driven Robert Hyde wild. His reticence and indifference apparently drained Robert Philips of all confidence and they rarely spoke, although Mary entreated her son to communicate with his father. Some sort of rapprochement must have followed because Robert Philips had overall charge of the mill at Calver in Derbyshire until it was abandoned in 1864. Here, Robert Hyde expresses his displeasure with his son in a letter about the Calver: 'You call me nervous and boast of your being a perfect financier. I keep strict accounts which you do not, and I know the incomings and accumulations where any and so forth and the responsibilities of my situation as a man of business . . .' In other words, you think you know it all and can even teach your very own father a thing or two. After the collapse of Calver, Robert Philips went into the Manchester business as a senior partner. He stayed there until 1871, when he chose to 'retire' to the Coles estate in Hertfordshire, becoming a gentleman farmer. Robert Hyde greeted this move with a seeming mixture of relief and disdain. He wrote:

> I have no doubt to become a country gentleman . . . would on the whole conduce to your comfort and happiness more than in remaining in business in Manchester. In the first place I don't think your turn of mind and general character suitable for business either for comfort and success and it makes it difficult for your partners to act harmoniously as partners should do . . .

Pretty much good riddance then. It seemed that Robert Hyde did love certain people fiercely – his mother Hannah, wife, Mary and his daughter, Caroline, while being a bit stingy with his affections regarding the others, including his sons. The death of his beloved Caroline aged only thirty-seven, must have been a huge blow. Only Henry Russell was held in any esteem, and yet it was his other son, Edward Hyde, who inherited Quarry Bank. Edward Hyde was described as being, 'an enigma, incurable vain and extravagant'. But, by then, the apprentice children, if not their descendants, were long gone. Robert Hyde died in 1875, aged seventy-nine. Henry Russell wrote to older brother Robert Philips who was then still residing in some luxury at Coles: 'I daresay you will miss Pater's coming to Coles and conferring on matters with him and also feeling that the cottage is quite deserted. Pater was certainly a most reliable rallying point and one always to be depended upon, giving stability to all around him.' The 'daresay' gives the game away. It is laden with doubt and uncertainty. It is often said to be a truism that sons don't appreciate their fathers until they're gone; maybe this was Henry Russell's slight dig at his absent older brother? Henry Russell went on to marry the heiress Emily Gair, but sadly insanity ran through the Gair family and Emily spent her life (or most of it) under potassium bromide and chloral hydrate to sedate her, very probably being bipolar. Henry had to write to and deal with their daughters on his own, because Emily often neglected to. It must have been a very lonely life.

⋆ ⋆ ⋆

The children finding themselves in the employ of the Gregs of Quarry Bank found many things to be grateful for. They were fed. They were educated, to an extent. They were eventually paid, if they made the grade. They were housed, at a cost. They were encouraged to settle in Styal. They weren't beaten. They were introduced to a religious way of looking at things. By examining the fabric of who Samuel and Hannah and their immediate family were, we can see why the apprentices were treated this way. It cannot be said that, given the mores of the time, Samuel and Hannah did not do their best to improve the lives of those who worked for them. However, later in the story of the legacy left by the Gregs and Quarry Bank, this was to come back and bite their own children, especially the unfortunate Samuel Jnr. Quarry Bank eventually found itself being run by Colonel Alec Greg, and we will deal with his tenure in the next chapter. But all that followed Samuel and Hannah's reign can be traced back to the way they treated their employees, especially the apprentice children. The future of the village, and of those who remained in Styal, was indelibly stamped with the Greg identity. In many ways they were part of an unconscious experiment in social history, creating a glorious anachronism.

CHAPTER TWELVE

Legacy

You only have to stroll around Styal village today to see the physical manifestation of part of Quarry Bank's legacy. Behind the immaculate trimmed hedgerows and impossibly neat gardens, there thrives a modern community, which still includes some descendants of millworkers. Now, though, their rubbish is not left to rot in open carts, it is trundled away in wheelie bins or recycled. The houses look the same, but have been modernised. They're warmer, they have proper sanitation, they don't house any more than three or four people, they have broadband. But, also, the village is full, the people have stayed, and it's the people who are the real legacy of the Greg family and their mill.

Did Hannah and Samuel consciously set out to impose their beliefs and aspirations on to the workers at Quarry Bank? Certainly Hannah seemed to have the reformist zeal of one who had all the privileges of a good education, reasonable wealth, a good marriage and a number of healthy children; and of someone who wanted to share their gifts out among the less privileged. We have tracked the various arguments she had with Samuel during their courtship, and presumably, after the 'twelvemonth' her sister Elizabeth advised was a decent period during which not to argue with your new husband, stopped biting her tongue. She railed against his views on charity and lectured him on Homer, yet never seemingly breathed a word in public about her abolitionist past and his connections to slaving, contrary to what appeared in the television series. Yet here they were, creating what some like John Doherty and Frederick Engels would say, was white slavery.

In the television series, Doherty is the Gregs' bête noire, as he was in real life. He dogged them all the way through the Ten Hour laws and beyond, all the time championing the right to freedom for all individuals, especially the downtrodden poor. He was there with Esther in her hour of need and he published pamphlets galore decrying the apprentice system and its abusers. Ironically, there was little Samuel could have done about his father Thomas's links with the slave trade, even if he'd had a mind to. But it must have always been there, between man and wife. The television series deals with this thorny issue in the fictional character of Peter, once Samuel is safely out of the way. Back in history, though, was there many a long evening when Hannah would chastise Samuel, in a way befitting a wife of that time, for his father's misdeeds? Were deals done? Hannah felt she had to compromise to succeed as Samuel's wife and as a mother to all their children. She put her personal development aside for some time and funnelled her love of all things intellectual into the pastoral care of her children and their education. She was also to do this with the apprentice children, apparently with Samuel's blessing. Was this. too, a compromise? There's nothing we can do about your father's slaves, but let's at least do what we can about our own?

When younger and still a Lightbody, Hannah wore her intellectual liberalism on her sleeve, later to add her education to it. She brandished these attributes, shield-like, to fend off the intellectually unworthy, and was probably responsible, together with her sisters, for earning the nickname 'the heavy Miss Lightbodies'. At times Hannah wanted nothing more than to be able to hold her head high, along with her family, and walk freely through society with nothing to be ashamed of and plenty to be proud of. Surely the treatment of the apprentice children fell into the category of 'We must do our very best'? All the more galling, then, to be harangued for dealing in the white slave trade by intellectuals and free thinkers they might have at one time called friends? Let's not be coy about this, the apprentice system was, at times, tantamount to a kind of slavery. The children had no choice; many were taken almost forcibly from their parents, who were unable to care for them adequately. Others were orphans who clung to whoever next walked through the door. They were then exposed to the greatest dangers and risks to their health, some for the rest of their lives, whether they were chewed up and spat out prematurely, or whether they worked until they dropped, their own children standing by to pick up their parents' yoke. Sure, they were supposedly free at eighteen, provided they could prove their age, but fines, lack of other opportunities and the relative comfort of steady employment kept them bound to the mill. Most had no other choice. That perceived freedom was nothing more than a phantom; when you tried to grasp at it, it simply dissolved through your fingers. It may equally be argued that this could be applied to most people's working lives. But then again, most people were not taken up as children, knowing no better.

When you look into the archived material that survives long after Samuel and Hannah passed away, something remarkable does begin to surface. An attitude, a singularity, an identity. Something unique to Quarry Bank and Styal, something almost indefinable. And it's present in the Oral Histories, the recorded interviews with some survivors of their time in the mill, conducted with village residents, some of whom were born as early as 1882. Of course, there's a Henshall there. In fact, there are two. Even Reg Worthington gets his say, and when you listen to the disembodied voices you can hear the very history of the place, echoing down through all those years.

As with Thomas Tonge's recollections, the Oral Histories offer a patchwork quilt of history, stories pieced together, intertwining, rewarding. And at this time, as far as the workers are concerned, the Greg family had come crashing down to earth from the heavens that once seemed to be their natural habitat.

The Apprentice House ceased to hold any apprentices after the abolition of the system in the mid-1800s. It became a private house and some people remember living there. Mrs

Hayman Slater, a niece of Samuel Henshall, the mill manager, recalls that she was actually born there. Mrs Slater gives us but a sliver of colour about a little-known Greg family member. There is scant knowledge of what happened to Beatrice Greg, daughter of Edward Hyde Greg and granddaughter of Robert Hyde Greg. Until, that is, you hear Mrs Slater tell of being carted around the village by an old lady in a donkey trap. Apparently the old woman was stone deaf and 'a crabby old so-and-so', known throughout the village as Miss B. Miss Beatrice Greg, that is. Ironically, given that she lived in the Apprentice House, Mrs Slater recalls living a life of 'comparative privilege'.

We've already heard what Emily Lyons, born 1901, had to say about her early sexual encounters, which wasn't a lot. However, she was more forthcoming on the subject of one Samuel Henshall: 'Sammy 'Enshall, he wanna much cop! Told me off for talkin'. Sometimes 'e'd get 'is 'air off – I was always in hot water . . .' Emily also had something to say about the wages: 'you couldn't get anythin' out of the Gregs . . .'

When Emily really warmed up she painted a somewhat bawdy picture of mill life in her time. She tells of singing together to pass the time when working, especially with someone named Gertie Garner. Once, she recalls, Annie Rounds threw a cop (a spindle of cotton) at Charlie Bailey, who was annoying her, but, 'he ducked and it hit Alec Greg'. Charlie was promptly sent home. One Christmas they all clubbed together for a bottle of whisky. Emily had never tasted whisky before, inevitably getting drunk, and ended up 'falling into a basket full of bobbins'. She reckoned that they were 'lucky we didn't get caught'. Emily applies that same degree of luck to not falling pregnant, because 'no one knew the facts of life . . .' No change there then.

Alice Brown, born 1898, had a family history at the mill going back as far as 1791, via her father, head overlooker, Tom Venables, and his family before him. Her softly spoken words speak volumes. Alice had her clothes made new for her once a year at Whit Week and was in the Girl Guides group run by Madge Greg. Madge was the daughter of Ernest William Greg and Marion Cross and was to prove to be the kind of great-great-granddaughter that Hannah would have approved of immensely. Alice speaks calmly of the time she spent in the Glee Club, singing at Norcliffe Hall, and of the time she heard about that baby being abandoned on 'some man's front steps in the village'. That baby who was taken to Wilmslow Police and never heard of again. She recalls with indignation the practice of Alec Greg shutting the mill gates in your face if you were but a second too late for work, no matter that you'd run all the way from Wilmslow! She also recalls teaching herself how to lip read, and how, when the millhands knew that Alec Greg was on the way, they'd twitch imaginary moustaches, mimicking him.

Alec Greg seems to have plenty on his hands during his tenure at Quarry Bank. Being mimicked, struck by flying cops, drunken lads and, apparently, pregnant girls. How times were changing. Alice tells of a lad, Billy, who was sweet on her. Billy was a piecer who clearly had more time on his hands than he knew what to do with. One day he tried to kiss Alice, who swiftly, and it seems accurately, threw a shuttle at him. Having such a deadly item thrown at you was a sure sign that your attentions were not going to be reciprocated and, suitably crestfallen, Billy kicked it back. It hit Alice on the shin, bringing up a lump that she still had in 1985.

Alice remembered the First World War all too well: ‘all the young men were called up in 1914’, and the women went to work on munitions in Burnage, where many learned that they’d lost their boyfriends. Alice didn’t lose a boyfriend – rather, she found one, by accident. She was on the train when she realised that she’d lost her ticket. The conductor phoned ahead to tell the station that a certain Alice Brown had indeed bought a ticket. Alice married him.

Joe Worthington’s granddad was the renowned Gresty, gamekeeper to Henry Philips Greg and Colonel Ernest, his cousin. This was around the late 1800s to the turn of the century. Gresty was held in high esteem by Henry, who ‘wouldn’t dream’ of leaving the house with a gun and without Gresty. Colonel Ernest was different, he did what he wanted. Gresty’s job was to patrol the perimeters and ‘see off undesirables . . .’ He was also obliged to go on many shoots with Henry, with whom he was able to enjoy a candid relationship. Like the time some idiot had let loose a tad too early for their liking. This particular idiot was actually a guest at the Hall. Old Henry must have sighed in resignation, ‘I suppose he’s seen off all the ducks . . . ?’ Gresty didn’t mince his words. ‘Aye, and they’ve tekken t’ruddy drakes wi’ ’em!’

Another outspoken person was around at the time of the estimable Gresty. This was a girl, although not directly descended from Esther Price (for all we know), who could certainly lay claim to have inherited Esther's mantle. Bertha Brown (née Silverwood) was the kind of girl who would have given Esther a real run for her money, if they'd been around at the same time and joined forces. In which case, Lord help the rest of the apprentices. Bertha was, in her own words, 'a beggar for the lads', which probably accounts for her reputation, as relayed by Florrie Downs to those lads who wanted to take her 'for a walk'. It wasn't that Bertha was put off by the 'wrong 'uns'. She once dated Alec Worthington, a butcher from Styal with a bad reputation himself. Bertha's dad apparently 'wiped the floor' with her mum for letting her go out, 'wi' scum like 'im!' Already I was beginning to see that Bertha would probably not have allowed her mum, or anyone, to have much say in what she did or did not do. She confesses to being a 'big girl' who youngsters went to if they were in a spot of bother. If they'd been bullied, Bertha was their go-to girl, and had her own way of dealing with the bullies – 'I tanned 'em, even the lads . . .' She once got in trouble for sticking some bully's head down an unflushed toilet (this time a girl). You clearly did not mess with Bertha, not even if you happened to be Bertha herself – she once set her own 'lovely hair' on fire when trying to bake potato cakes.

In the same way that Esther had stood up to the Gregs, Bertha would follow suit, maybe with a little less in the way of righteousness but a whole lot of sass. Bertha wore 'enormous knickers', which she hated. They were only good for one thing, scrumping for pears. It was on such a scrumping mission that they were spotted by no less than a young Alec Greg, who gave chase. Bertha needed a head start as her knickers were stuffed with pears. And so she ran, hitching up her skirts and scattering pears as she went. It would be to no avail. Later Alec Greg recalled, 'I don't know why the devil Bertha Silverwood ran, I could tell her with her fat legs.' Thirty or forty years before, James Sparkes had been shot at for less.

One day in May 1822, two members of the Greg family, probably Hannah and Samuel, had approached a new and nervous Job Baker and had enquired about the vulnerable boy's place of origin. The well-dressed gentry had received an embarrassed stuttering reply for their troubles and the young boy had fled from their daunting presence. Fast forward about a hundred years and a similarly impressive adult, going by the name of Greg, approaches a somewhat stout girl, possibly sporting slightly singed hair.

'What's your name?'

'Mary Jane.'

'Where do you live?'

'Down the grid.'

'You're a naughty girl!'

A cheeky schoolyard rhyme. Downright impudence, or someone confident in who they are and where they stand in the world?

Bertha attended Oak School and benefited from the kind of education Hannah had always wanted for the children of the mill and the village. Sometimes, though, the classes received a little more than they had anticipated and dared not have hoped for. The head of the school at the time was Philip Bracegirdle and you did well not to be seated in the first three rows of his class for he had an unfortunate tendency to spit when he spoke. Mr Bracegirdle seemingly held the same beliefs as Samuel Greg's Greek master, Mr Parr, as he was liable to 'cane scholars at will'. He also taught in rhyme, which must have been something of a novelty to help the children through the day, unless you were in the first three rows of course. Mr Bracegirdle apparently had a neighbour with whom he did not get on, to such a degree that on one particular day the neighbour came into school and 'belted' Mr Bracegirdle. A fight of sorts ensued and Bertha said the class 'didn't know who to shout for . . .' Mr Bracegirdle wasn't the one to settle things, but apparently he knew someone who would. He ran into the class of a Miss Parker, who reputedly had a moustache. Miss Parker saw the neighbour off, 'giving him a good shaking'. The class were enthralled – 'she were a big woman, a suffragette . . .'

Bertha talks proudly of her dad, Dick Silverwood. Dick was something of a horse-whisperer, before there was a name for them. She remembers fondly, and with some awe, the day he chased after a spooked horse, which was clattering out of control and pulling a gun carriage while two young soldiers, out of their depth, watched on, powerless. Dick ran alongside the horse, speaking softly in its ear, until it calmed and slowed and he gained control of the reins.

In those days, holidays were actually taken, sometimes away from Styal and the mill. It's credited to the newly installed railway system, but these were people who wanted to leave the valley. They wanted life outside what they knew and sometimes they were awed by what they found. Bessie Smith relates being offered a break from her toil by her husband, who wanted to take her to the Lakes. Bessie was somewhat unmoved. 'Me, in the country all the time and I want a bit o' life!' It was Blackpool or nothing for Bessie. Bertha may well have been on that same trip, for she recalls reaching the end of a trip and standing, looking out across the dunes and the sand, with her dad, when they both saw the sea for the first time. Dick Silverwood sighed and spoke to her. 'In't that a great big pit . . . ?'

The Gregs of these times were changing too. Margaret Hyde Greg, known as Madge to Alice Brown and her other Girl Guides, served as a nurse in the First World War. She was on the front line intermittently between 1914 and 1918 at Ypres and the Somme. Madge showed great courage and was a leader at just over twenty years old, refusing to panic when a fresh load of wounded poured in one day, catching them without beds ready or available. She took charge and knocked up trestles out of spare boxes. Her two brothers also served during these campaigns, Arthur Tylston and Robert Philips. Arthur had been shot in the face during one land assault and remembered falling to the ground spitting what turned out to be his own teeth. He was laid up in a makeshift military hospital bed when Madge managed to get time off to visit him. She recalls that he couldn't speak to her because he'd lost part of his jaw, so she did all the talking. She'd been assured of his recovery and said her goodbyes. Arthur was still only nineteen years old when he was declared fit for duty. After a raid he was flying home when he was shot between the eyes and killed instantly. Their one-way conversation in the hospital was to have been their last. Arthur left a fiancée back in England, who was distraught and wrote some absolutely heart-breakingly moving poetry, still in the archives at Quarry Bank.

Brother Robert also died in France, and Ernest and Marian Greg must have prayed they'd not lose Madge too. Somewhere in between her brothers' deaths, Madge returned to the Somme. She was tending to shell-shocked patients, those hollow-eyed ghosts, when there was an attack. Only this time, it wasn't the Germans Madge had to defend herself from. A deranged patient attacked her, blackening an eye and bruising her cheek. She was given a day off. Later, when she was suffering from exhaustion, a wounded foot became septic and she was given more time off. These breaks from the horror possibly saved her life and she returned after the war to marry a surgeon and become a doctor in her own right. Hannah Greg would indeed have been proud.

Madge's youngest brother was lucky enough to have been born too late to serve in that awful war, and it was also his dubious privilege to oversee the final days of Quarry Bank Mill as a going concern of the Greg family. It was Alexander Carlton Greg, born 1902, who chased Bertha and her pear-stuffed knickers through his own woods. It was probably Alec who was given such rhyming cheek by said Bertha. It was certainly Alec Greg who bequeathed the bulk of the estate to the National Trust in 1939. He wanted to be a fruit farmer, following a long line of Greg children who didn't see the mill business as their own, something that was a bone of contention between Hannah and Samuel.

Reg Worthington tells many stories about Quarry Bank and Styal and it speaks volumes for the kind of people the Greg legacy of employment had engendered. It could be said that the encouragement of free speech and free thought led to people taking the Gregs at their word – look at Bertha Silverwood. Some, however, took it all a little bit further. Allegedly Colonel Alec was in the habit of expecting his people to bow as he passed, something his ancestors had enjoyed throughout their lives, and something he'd seen afforded to his own parents. However, insurrection was in the air and one of the volleys came from his very own Unitarian minister, Voysey. One day, in his pulpit at Norcliffe, Voysey was heard to preach of Alec, that 'he expects that all the birds in the trees ought to tweet good morning'. As part of his seemingly patrician behaviour Alec was also wont to turn up at the houses of his villagers and just walk in, expecting to be fed potato cakes. He'd have done better to have paid heed to the story of an earlier Greg doing such a thing with John Brown the gamekeeper and the effortlessly offensive Mrs Scott. After hearing from Reg of one such potato cake visitation whilst she was out, Nora Worthington grabbed the young Reg by the wrist and they marched round to see Alec, where Nora, 'gave him what for . . .' Reg was thrilled. Perhaps the worst example of the mounting lack of respect for the master was the one that must have cut Colonel Alec to the quick. Once, when making his way through the village, Alec and his companion passed by a group of demobbed soldiers. Alec was not to get his expected bow. He audibly complained that 'even they do not salute me . . .' He did get his reply though. They told him to 'fuck off!'

Was this just an expression of freedom of thought and expression without fear? It was certainly meant to express contempt, but was it simply aimed at Alec because he was there? Would any Greg have suffered the same insult? The people of Quarry Bank had evolved into a free-thinking, fearless body of people who also expressed themselves just as freely. They had outgrown their honorary status as the white slaves of Britain and they would bow to no man. At this point I want to quote someone who, as a character in the television series, and in real life too, had been a major part of the Greg and Quarry Bank history:

> I want to better the condition of the people – to have them stand erect, and look boldly in the faces of their masters, and to tell them, 'We are not your slaves; we are your equals.' We are one side of the bargain, you are only the other. We give you an equivalent for what we get from you, and are therefore entitled to, at the least, equal respect.

A fitting comment on the people who grew into what we witnessed as the legacy of Quarry Bank Mill? When he spoke those words in 1831, little did John Doherty know he would be describing the descendants of the workers at Quarry Bank. Could he lay justifiable claim to have freed these 'slaves' as part of his campaigning life? Or did they free themselves, with a gentle but persistent push in the back from the likes of Hannah, Samuel and their children? The answer probably lies somewhere in between: one allowed it, one pursued it. What we do know for certain is the legacy of Quarry Bank and its apprentice children can be felt today, and that what they sacrificed should not be forgotten and not mourned, but remembered with pride and, above all, celebrated.

Index